PELICAN BOOKS

DIGGING UP THE PAST

Sir Leonard Woolley received his university training at New College, Oxford, and afterwards became Assistant Keeper in the Ashmolean Museum. He went with the Eckley B. Coxe Expedition to Nubia from 1907 to 1911, and was in charge of the British Museum Excavations at Carchemish until 1914. During the war of 1914–18 he did intelligence staff work in Egypt, and received the Croix de Guerre. He was a prisoner in Turkey for two years until the war was over, when he became Political Officer in North Syria. He was in the Intelligence Department from 1939, and from 1943 was Archaeological Adviser to the War Office, responsible for the protection of the monuments of art and history in war areas.

From 1922 to 1934 he conducted the excavations at Ur for the Trustees of the British Museum and the Museum of the University of Pennsylvania. In 1935 he began an excavation in the Hatay near Antioch, in the hope of tracing further the relations between the civilization of Greece and of the East, and in particular to find out whether such relations existed between the earliest European civilization, that of Crete, and the old cultural centres such as the Mesopotamian, and also the Hittite.

He was given the honorary degrees of D.Litt. by Trinity College, Dublin, and of LL.D. by the University of St Andrews, and was an F.S.A., honorary A.R.I.B.A., Huxley Medallist for 1942, Lucy Wharton Drexel Medallist for 1955, and James Bryce Memorial Lecturer for 1949. His *Ur of the Chaldees* and *A Forgotten Kingdom* have been published as Pelicans, and he was the author of a King Penguin entitled *Ur: The First Phases*. He died in 1960.

Sir Leonard Woolley

DIGGING UP
THE PAST

PENGUIN BOOKS

BALTIMORE · MARYLAND

Penguin Books Ltd, Harmondsworth, Middlesex, England
Penguin Books Inc., 7110 Ambassador Road, Baltimore, Maryland 21207, U.S.A.
Penguin Books Australia Ltd, Ringwood, Victoria, Australia

—

First published by Ernest Benn 1930
Published in Pelican Books 1937
Reprinted 1949, 1950, 1952, 1954, 1956
Second edition published by Ernest Benn, 1954
Published in Pelican Books 1960
Reprinted 1961, 1963, 1965, 1967, 1970, 1972

—

Copyright © the Estate of Leonard Woolley, 1930, 1954

Made and printed in Great Britain
by Hunt Barnard & Co. Ltd,
Aylesbury, Bucks.
Set in Monotype Caslon
Collogravure plates by Harrison & Sons Ltd

AUTHOR'S NOTE

This little book is based on a series of six
talks broadcast by the BBC, to whom I
am indebted for permission to re-publish
the substance in permanent form

62681

Preface to the Second Edition

THIS book was first published in 1930 and when Messrs Ernest Benn proposed that in this edition it should be brought up to date I imagined that to do so after a lapse of nearly a quarter of a century would involve a great deal of work. Actually this has not been the case. If I had been dealing with the results of field archaeology most of the chapters would have had to be re-written, for in almost every field the last twenty years have seen so great an advance in our knowledge that there are few conclusions arrived at in the 1920s which do not need modification today – the facts remain, but they have to be re-interpreted in the light of new facts. But *Digging up the Past* dealt with principles and methods, and these change little if at all. I had not, in those early days, said a great deal about the use of air photography, which has become one of the most potent weapons of field archaeology, but writers far more qualified than I, such as O. G. S. Crawford, have written fully on the subject, and I can perhaps plead that since it is not so much a part of digging as a preliminary to it I may be excused from quoting them at length. There are now new methods of dating objects, by dendrochronology and by the radioactivity of carbon; however useful they may prove they have nothing to do with digging as such; the digger may supply the material but it is for the scientist in his laboratory to practise the method. The additions which I have made are all in character with the book as originally written, the purpose of which was to explain

5

to the layman the kind of work that the field archaeologist does and why he does it. Some necessary aspects of that work I have merely referred to in passing – for instance, the writing of field notes and the cataloguing of objects – partly because they can be taken for granted, partly because every excavator employs – or should employ – the system which best suits himself and there is no hard-and-fast formula to be generally observed; we make our notes, each of us, for our own use, and the particular form which they take is of no interest to anyone else. I have tried throughout to make it clear that archaeology is a very human science; if we constrict the archaeologist in the strait-waistcoat of what has been called 'method-ology' he will be only too apt to lose that human element which is the sole justification of his being. Of course, objects must be catalogued and the catalogue must record measurements and material, form, colour, technique and, perhaps, chemical composition; but never forget that the object was made by an in-dividual man who was not bothering about any such analysis but was a creator giving shape to an idea. The archaeologist's job is to get through the object to its maker; if he does that then, helped by the material qualities of the thing, he will begin to understand the society in which the thing's maker lived. Anybody can dig up things; but it is only by observation and interpre-tation that we can dig up the past.

L.W.

Contents

CONTENTS

List of Illustrations

11. The Palace of Minos at Knossos. Restoration of the actual building. (*a*) Room of the Priest-King. (*b*) Stepped porch and central staircase. *By permission of Sir Arthur Evans.*

12. Plan of the 'model village' for workmen at el-Amarna. *By courtesy of the Egypt Exploration Society.*

13. A temple at el-Amarna. (*a*) The ground plan as found. (*b*) The ground plan as restored.

14. A temple at el-Amarna. Suggested restoration of the ruined building whose actual remains are shown in Pl. 13.

15. A private chapel in a house at Ur showing the altar, the raised pavement of the chancel, and in the foreground the burial vault below the floor.

16. Palace of Minos at Knossos. Reconstruction of the actual remains. *By permission of Sir Arthur Evans.*

17. The 'parlour' of a workman's house at el-Almarna. *By courtesy of the Egypt Exploration Society.*

18. Inlaid gold coffin for viscera. Tomb of Tutankhamen. *By permission of the Griffith Institute, Oxford.*

19. The 'tomb-chapel' over the entrance of a tomb at Karanog, with its brickwork undisturbed. *By courtesy of the Trustees of the University Museum, Philadelphia.*

20. Part of a log coffin of the Bronze Age from a Scandinavian peat-bog showing the body with all the garments preserved.

21. A pre-dynastic cemetery in Southern Egypt, showing the close-set grave hollows in the sand. *By courtesy of the Department of Antiquities, Egyptian Government.*

22. 'Cleaned for photographing'. Two pre-dynastic Egyptian graves with skeletons and objects in position. *By courtesy of the Department of Antiquities, Egyptian Government.*

CHAPTER I

Introductory

*

BEFORE I begin to describe the methods of
Field Archaeology it might be as well to say
something about its aims. Nobody supposes that
the digging up of antiquities is in itself a scientific end, and though there is always a thrill
attending the discovery of buried treasure the
ever-growing interest of the public in archaeological work is by no means limited to its
dramatic accidents; behind the mere romance
there is something of real and enduring value.

It is difficult at first to get in proper perspec-
tive such discoveries as those of Tutankhamen's
tomb, of the Palace of Minos in Crete, and of the
royal tombs at Ur; isolated by their novelty they
come out of focus and dazzle us, but later they
withdraw and, linking up with other things in
the field of ordered vision, become features in
the historical background against which, con-
sciously or unconsciously, we play our part.

When Schliemann found the treasures of Mycenae what first startled the world was his belief that Homer's poems had been proved to be literally true: now few would argue whether or not in those tombs lay the bodies of Agamemnon and Clytemnestra masked with gold, but no one thinks of Homer or of the beginnings of Greek history without having at the back of his mind the picture of Mycenaean pomp and beauty.

In these days natural science is unfolding before us a panorama which to our great-grand-fathers seemed in its beginnings blasphemous: to them it undermined the foundations of belief, to us it establishes thought upon a base broader and more rational. Science reckons time in millions of years and stretches space to infinity; the wider outlook does not make us one bit less interested in the things of today and tomorrow, and may seem scarcely to affect our practice, but it is there, part of our consciousness, and the more it is explored the better we can understand ourselves. Archaeology is doing the same thing in a smaller field: it deals with a period limited to a few thousand years and its subject is not the universe, not even the human race, but modern man. We dig, and say of these pots and pans, these beads and weapons, that they date back to 3000 or 4000 B.C., and the on-looker is tempted to exclaim at their age, and to admire them simply because they are old. Their real interest lies in the fact that they are new. If mere age be the standard, all that we unearth is insignificant compared to the dinosaur's fossil egg, and, for that matter, what is six thousand years in the life of the human race when we have to calculate that in terms of geological periods? The importance of our archaeological material is that it throws light on the history of men very like ourselves, on a civilization which is bound up with that of today.

We cannot divorce ourselves from our past; we are always conscious of precedents, not least so when we flout them, and we let experience shape our views and actions: this is so much the case that when tradition is absent or crystallizes into unreasoned convention, as it has done with the Australian Bushmen, progress stops. But the past to which we appeal must be in a sense our own, precedents set by men conditioned much as we are, the experience of races or individuals morally akin to us; its value is proportionate to the degree of continuity by which we are linked to it.

The political thinker of a hundred years ago would cite his parallels and draw his arguments from the Roman or Greek world, finding that cognate with his own, but there he stopped short; Greek civilization presented itself to him as something born full-grown with no history behind it, giving little opportunity for observing development and cause. Today we can see that modern man did not begin his career in 500 B.C., nor even perhaps in 5000 B.C.; from the flower of Attic culture we can work back and find the roots spreading far afield, and sending up perennial blossoms all differing with the nature of the soil and the tending they have received, but all of one stock, and in the light of such knowledge we can better judge and control the present and the future growth. And this enlightenment is not merely for the specialist, for the research student in history. The opening-up of the world affects us all, becomes part of the general intellectual inheritance, and the justification of archaeology is that it does in the end concern everyone. Its direct appeal is due to the fact that, compared with natural science, it comes with simpler introductions. Its subject is modern man, not a universe which resolves itself more and more into an intellectual abstraction, and its material is the work of man's hands. We see the elaborate drainage-system of Knossos and at once feel at home; the cosmetics found in an ancient grave strike us as pathetically up to date; the surprise which a visitor to a Museum expresses at the age of a given object is in exact proportion to his recognition of the object's essential modernity – it is the surprise of one who sees his horizon suddenly opening out; and the advantage of archaeology is that it offers Darien peaks so many and so easy to climb.

*

I was led to write the above by being told that the first question which the reader would like to have answered might be, 'Why does anyone dig?' and that came as a shock, for it has seemed to me so obvious that the purpose of archaeology is to illustrate and to discover the course of human civilization, which is certainly an end worth while. But it might be urged that the question is specifically confined to Field Archaeology, whereas the course of civilization is the subject of history: that being so, if the historian uses as his material those relics of the past which the field archaeologist does, as a matter of fact, bring to light, could not the material be produced by casual digging? Is there any justification for a person who claims to be an expert in a specialized branch of science and then does in an elaborate way what the labourer could do much more cheaply?

If that is what the question means – and it could mean a good many things – it betrays complete ignorance of what Field Archaeology is. In its essence Field Archaeology is the application of scientific method to the excavation of ancient objects, and it is based on the theory that the historical value of an object depends not so much on the nature of the object itself as on its associations, which only scientific excavation can detect. The casual digger and the plunderer aim at getting something of artistic or commercial value, and there their interest stops. The archaeologist, being after all human, does enjoy finding rare and beautiful objects, but wants to know all about them, and in any case prefers the acquisition of knowledge to that of things; for him digging consists very largely in observation, recording and interpretation. There is all the difference in the world between the purpose and the methods of the scientific worker and those of the robber; it remains to be seen whether there is a corresponding difference in the value of the work done. Really the whole of this book is an attempt to explain the means which the archaeologist adopts, and to prove that they do achieve the end in view, but it may be as well to clear the ground in advance by showing to how great an extent the historical value of an object depends on our knowledge of the conditions in which it was found.

Supposing that a peasant somewhere or other unearths a marble statue or a gold ornament; he sells it, and it passes from hand to hand until from a dealer's shop it makes its way into a museum or a private collection. By this time nobody knows where it was found or how, it has been torn from its context and can be judged only as a thing in itself; its quality as a work of art does not suffer, but how about its historical value? Experts have to guess, from such knowledge as they already possess, to what country and age it belongs, and if they agree the statue or cup is assumed to illustrate further that particular known phase of art; very likely they will not agree, and it becomes merely a bone of contention for the learned, and a source of confusion for the layman. If the object found be, for instance, a clay pot having no claim to artistic merit, then, stripped of any significance it might have possessed as a historical document, it becomes absolutely valueless; if the finding of an important object be incorrectly reported it becomes a positive stumbling-block to science. Some Arabs, digging in the ruins of a Syrian church, discover by chance a silver goblet adorned with figures in relief, amongst them some which can credibly be identified as Christ and his apostles. Through various hands it passes to America. The dealers are ready with the story that it was discovered at Antioch, and 'the disciples were called Christians first at Antioch'; and the world is assured that here is the Holy Grail, the actual chalice of the Last Supper, bearing contemporary portraits of the apostles of Christ; and though the goblet was, in fact, found more than a hundred miles away from Antioch, and though, judging from its style, it must have been made at least 300 years after Christ's death, it is hard to dispel an error which has already gained a hearing and has so dramatic a ring. In this particular case the harm done to science was less because the story told was demonstrably false, and the purpose of it was clearly interested; many people might be deceived, but the expert was not obliged to recast his knowledge, gained from innumerable dated objects, of the art of the first four Christian centuries; but where the background of definite knowledge is slight an object robbed of its context may be a snare even to the expert. I recall the case of a bronze figure of a lion purchased in China; presumably it was Chinese, but to a certain scholar it seemed to present analogies with the very few such monuments that we possess of Hittite art; he declared it to be Hittite, and then made it the criterion for judging other works of art whose Hittite origin could not be disputed. Here subjective criticism based on too partial knowledge was to blame, but had anything been recorded as to the conditions of the lion's finding we should have been spared so much confusion in the history of Near Eastern art.

On the other hand an object of no value in itself may become a historical document of the greatest importance just because its associations have been properly observed. The great stone ruins of Zimbabwe, in Rhodesia, had long been a puzzle, and the wildest theories were current about them – they had been built by the Phoenicians, they were the Ophir from which Solomon obtained his gold, they were an outpost of ancient Egypt; and observe that if any one of these theories had been proved correct we should have had to revise very thoroughly our views of ancient history. A worthless scrap of Chinese porcelain found in the foundations of the buildings, but found in the course of a scientific excavation properly controlled, proves that the so-called temple is Medieval in date, and must be native African in authorship. A speculator digging for profit would never have bothered about that little potsherd nor, if he had, would anyone have paid any attention to it, for the very good reason that his methods would not have been such that his discoveries could have been accepted as scientific evidence: found as it was, it not only knocked falsehood on the head but opened up a new chapter in African history.

Treasure-hunting is almost as old as Man, scientific archaeology is a modern development, but in its short life of about seventy years it has done marvels. Thanks to excavation, thousands of years of human history are now familiar which a hundred years ago were a total blank, but this is not all, perhaps not even the most important part. The old histories, resting principally on written documents, were largely confined to those events which at every age writers thought most fit to record – wars, political happenings, the chronicles of kings – with such side-lights as could be gleaned from the literature of the time. The digger may produce more written records, but he also brings to light a mass of objects illustrating the arts and handicrafts of the past, the temples in which men worshipped, the houses in which they lived, the setting in which their lives were spent; he supplies the material for a social history of a sort that could never have been undertaken before. Until Schliemann dug at Mycenae, and Sir Arthur Evans in Crete, no one guessed that there had been a Minoan civilization. Not a single written word has been found to tell of it, yet we can trace the rise and fall of the ancient Minoan power, can see again the splendours of the Palace of Minos, and imagine how life was lived alike there and in the crowded houses of the humbler folk. The whole history of Egypt has been recovered by archaeological work, and that in astonishing detail; I suppose we know more about ordinary life in Egypt in the fourteenth century before Christ than we do about that of England in the fourteenth century A.D. To the spade we owe our knowledge of the Sumerians and the Hittites, great empires whose very existence had been forgotten, and in the case of other ancient peoples, the Babylonians and the Assyrians, the dry bones of previously known fact have had life breathed into them by the excavation of buried sites. It is a fine list of achievements, and it might be greatly expanded; all over Europe, in Central America, in China and in Turkestan excavation is supplementing our knowledge, and adding new vistas to our outlook over man's past; and to what is it all due? Not to the mere fact that antique objects have been dug out of the ground, but to their having been dug out scientifically.

But before I describe methods there is another point arising out of that first question 'Why does anyone dig?' People sometimes put the accent in a different place, and ask 'Why does anyone *dig*? Why do they have to use the spade to achieve these admirable results? How does it come about that things get buried and have to be dug up?'

Clearly, in the case of graves, which yield many of the archaeologist's treasures, the question does not arise, for the things were put underground deliberately and have remained there; but how do houses and cities sink below

the earth's surface? They do not: the earth rises
above them, and though people do not recognize the fact, it is happening all around them
every day. Go no further than London. How
many steps does one have to go down to enter
the Temple Church? Yet it stood originally at
ground level. The mosaic pavements of Roman
Londinium lie twenty-five to thirty feet below
the streets of the modern City. Wherever a
place has been continuously occupied the same
thing has happened. In old times municipal
scavenging did not amount to much, the street
was the natural receptacle for refuse and the
street level gradually rose with accumulated
filth; if it was re-paved the new cobbles were
laid over the old dirt, at a higher level, and you
stepped down into the houses on either side.
When a house was pulled down and rebuilt the
site would be partly filled in, and the new
ground floor set at or above street level; the
foundations of the older building would remain
undisturbed below ground. The process would
be repeated time after time so that when
foundations are made for the huge buildings of
today which go down nearly as far into the
earth as they rise into the air, the excavating
gangs cut through layer after layer of wall

stumps and artificial filling of which each represents a stage in the city's growth. In the Near East the rate of rise is faster. The commonest building material is mud brick, and mud brick walls have to be thick; when they collapse the amount of debris is very great, and fills the rooms to a considerable height, and as you cannot use mud bricks twice over, and the carting away of rubbish is expensive, the simplest course is to level the surface of the ruins and build on the top of them – which has the further advantage that it raises your new mud-brick building out of reach of the damp. In Syria and in Iraq every village stands on a mound of its own making, and the ruins of an ancient city may rise a hundred feet above the plain, the whole of that hundred feet being composed of superimposed remains of houses, each represented by the foot or so of standing wall which the collapse of the upper part buried and protected from destruction.

But what happens when a site is no longer inhabited? A Roman camp, for instance, occupied by the legionaries and abandoned after a few years – how does that get buried? Here we have Nature to thank. I remember how, when the L.C.C. cleared the slum area where

Bush House stands today, the heaps of broken brickwork and loose mortar were in the following year entirely hidden by a mass of purple willow-herb, and people used to take bus rides down the Strand just for the pleasure of looking over the high hoarding at this miracle of wild flowers. That happened in the space of a few months; had the 'island site' been left undisturbed for as many years, coarse turf would have covered the mounds and the ruins of Booksellers' Row would have been buried like those of Silchester. And if this can happen in the heart of London, how much more so in the country, where Nature fights at close range?

I have not mentioned one way in which buildings may be buried, because it is so lamentably rare; that is by volcanic action. If the field archaeologist had his will, every ancient capital would have been overwhelmed by the ashes of a conveniently adjacent volcano. It is with a green jealousy that the worker on other sites visits Pompeii and sees the marvellous preservation of its buildings, the houses standing up to the second floor, the frescoes on the walls, and all the furniture and household objects still in their places as the owners left them when they fled from the disaster. Failing a volcano, the best thing that can happen to a city, archaeologically speaking, is that it should be sacked and very thoroughly burnt by an enemy. The owners are not in a position to carry anything away and the plunderers are only out after objects intrinsically valuable, the fire will destroy much, but by no means everything, and will bring down on the top of what does remain so much in the way of ashes and broken brickwork that the survivors, if there are any, will not trouble to dig down into the ruins; a burnt site is generally a site undisturbed. It is where cities have decayed slowly that least is to be found in their ruins; the impoverished inhabitants will have pulled down the older buildings to re-use the material in their own hovels, they will make nothing good of their own and they will certainly leave nothing behind them when at last they desert the place; the top levels of such a site generally produce therefore few objects, and not much history except the melancholy history of decadence.

Granted, then, that things do get buried in one or other of these ways, how, it may be asked, do you set to work to find them? Why do you dig just where you do?

Burial does not always mean obliteration, and

there are generally some surface signs to guide
the digger. In the Near East no one could
possibly mistake the great mounds or 'tells'
which rose above the plain to mark the sites of
ancient cities; very often, if the place was an
important one, it can be identified from literary
sources even before excavation begins; the difficulty is rather which point of attack to choose
in so great an area. In Mesopotamia the highest
mound will probably conceal the Ziggurat or
staged tower attached to the chief temple;
sometimes a low-lying patch will betray the
position of the temple itself. Herodotus, visiting
Egypt in the fifth century B.C., remarked that
the temples there always lay in a hollow; the
reason was that while the mud-brick houses of
the town were shortlived and new buildings
constructed over the ruins of the old quickly
raised the ground level, the temples, built of
stone and kept always in good repair, outlived
many generations and remained at the same
level throughout; on an Egyptian site, therefore, a square depression ringed about by
mounds of crumbling grey brick gives the
excavator a very obvious clue. Earthworks are
enduring things, and the site, for instance, of a
Roman camp in Britain can nearly always be

traced by the low grass-clad lines of its ramparts, and the round barrows of the old British dead are still clear to see upon the Downs; but even where there is nothing upstanding, surface indications may not be lacking. In a dry summer the grass withers more quickly where the soil lies thin over the buried tops of stone walls, and I have seen the entire plan of a Roman villa spread out before me where no spade had ever dug; darker lines in a field of growing corn or, in the very early morning, a difference of tone given by the dew on the blades, will show where buildings run underground: nowadays air photographs bring to light masses of evidence invisible to one who stands upon the ground. An air photograph gives us the whole layout of the Roman village of Caistor, so that the excavator can confidently select the particular building he would like to dig, whereas, before, the site of Caistor was unknown; even more remarkable is it that an air photograph discovered Woodhenge, and showed on the plain surface of ploughed fields the concentric rings of dots where thousands of years ago wooden posts had been planted. From the ground such things are often quite invisible, or visible only at some lucky moment. At Wadi Halfa, in the northern

Sudan, MacIver and I had dug a temple and part of the Egyptian town, but, search the desert as we might for two months, we had failed to find any trace of the cemetery which must have been attached to the place. One evening we climbed a little hill behind the house to watch the sunset over the Nile; we were grumbling at our ill luck when suddenly MacIver pointed to the plain at our feet; its whole surface was dotted with dark circles which, though we had tramped over it day after day, we had never seen. I ran down the hill and the circles vanished as I came close to them but, guided by MacIver from above, I made little piles of gravel here and there, one in the middle of each ring; and when we started digging there next morning our Arab workmen found under each pile the square, rock-cut shaft of a tomb. The original grave-diggers had heaped the splinters of stone round the mouth of the shaft, and when they filled it up again a certain amount remained over; 4000 years had produced a dead level of stone and gravel where the eye could distinguish no difference of arrangement or texture; but for the space of five minutes in the day the sun's rays, coming at a particular angle, brought out a darker tint in the stone which had been quarried from deeper underground – but, even so, the effect could be seen only from above, and perhaps from a single point.

The archaeologist, in fact, has to keep his eyes open for evidence of all sorts. At Carchemish, in North Syria, my old Greek foreman, Gregori, an experienced digger if ever there was one, and I, completely mystified our Turkish inspector. We told him we were going to excavate a cemetery, and as we had not previously found graves he was duly interested, and asked to be shown the spot. We took him outside the earth ramparts of the old city to a ploughed field by the river bank, lying fallow that year, and, pointing to the fragments of pottery which strewed the ground, explained that these constituted good evidence for the existence of a graveyard. Then Gregori and I, consulting together, started to make piles of stones marking the position of individual graves. This was too much for Fuad Beg, who protested that we were bluffing him; I betted that we should find a grave under every pile and no graves at all except where we had put a mark; he took the bet and lost it, and spent a month wondering why. It was really a simple case of deduction.

The river bank was of hard gravel, the made soil overlying it very shallow, and disturbed to the depth of only about three inches by the feeble Arab plough; the field, being fallow, was covered with sparse growth, for the most part shallow-rooted, but with a mixture of sturdier weeds of a sort whose roots go deeply down; if one looked carefully it became manifest that these weeds were sometimes single, but often in clumps of four or five plants, but a clump never measured more than six feet across; at some time or another the gravel subsoil had been broken up, so that the plant roots could penetrate it, and it had been broken up in patches which would be just the right size for graves; the broken pottery on the surface represented either shallow burials or, more probably, offerings placed above the graves at ground level, and every deep-growing weed or group of weeds meant a grave-shaft. The deduction proved correct.

In just the same way Professor van Riet Lowe has remarked that in Rhodesia and the Transvaal a quite distinctive flora grows on sites which the ancients used as dumps for rubbish and he tells a story* *a propos* of this. At Zim-

*I quote here from O. G. S. Crawford's admirable book *Archaeology in the Field*, p. 264.

babawe 'we were standing on the Acropolis and looking down upon the Valley of Ruins I noticed (through my binoculars) an area covered by grass and a particularly unpleasant thorny ground-creeper with masses of small yellow flowers, and indicating this, said "There is a large midden" . . . . When we had descended into the valley we went on to my entirely un-inviting patch and judiciously cleared and dug into a few small areas from every one of which we extracted handfuls of potsherds encased in ash.'

The evidence may be something less material than grass and weeds. Towards the end of my first season's work at Atchana in North Syria I said to my foreman 'Hamoudi, I've always said that this must be a royal city; we've dug out some very good private houses, but before we close down we ought to do a bit of work on the palace; it would be nice to prove the point.' Hamoudi concurred heartily. 'You know where it is, don't you?' I asked. Hamoudi was quite taken aback; 'Of course I do; don't you?' 'Yes. Just go along and mark out a square that we can clear in ten days.' He did so, and I went to look and agreed that he was right on top of the palace but suggested that as we could excavate so little of it in the time left to us it would be best to get part of the façade, and I shifted his square a few yards to the south-east. We dug down, and came straight on the front steps of the royal palace with its columned portico and entrance-chamber. Now this was not magic or second sight. We were working on a long high mound whose axis ran north-west by south-east; in its heyday it had been a city enclosed by great walls (this was really the acropolis, there had probably been a lower town as well) and the mound's top had been crowded with close-built houses, and with the smoke of their charcoal cooking-stoves and with the very primitive methods of sanitation employed and the heat of the Syrian summer sun the atmosphere must have been, to say the least of it, most unpleasant. The mound rose highest at the north-west end. In the summer the prevailing wind blows from the north-west, from the Anti-Taurus mountains which are capped with snow almost the year round. Obviously the most agreeable site for a house was where you got the benefit of a cool breeze and the wind carried away from you all the smells of the huddled town; that was the site the King was bound to choose: and since the palace needed protection the barracks or castle would be close by where it had too the advantage of commanding the road that ran inland from the sea-coast, and those solid buildings would account for the greater height of the mound at this end. It was a matter of common sense and of human nature, which changes very little; in the plain round Atchana there are mounds still occupied, and invariably the landlord's stone-built house is at the north-west end and the reed or mud huts of his labourers lie to the south-east.

It was deduction of another sort that led to the discovery of Tutankhamen's tomb. The Valley of the Kings at Thebes contained the known graves of all the Pharaohs of the Eighteenth Dynasty except two: clearly it was the burial-ground of the dynasty, therefore *all* the kings of that dynasty ought to have been found there, and since they had not, the missing ones were still to seek, but to seek within the valley confines. For three years the late Lord Carnarvon worked in that part of the valley which was still unexplored, shifting the thousands of tons of limestone chips which filled the bottom of the ravine, scraping the cliff sides in search of a possible doorway, and it was only when the wearisome task was well-nigh done that the

astonishing discovery was made: he and Howard
Carter owed their success not to a stroke of
good luck but to the patient following-out of a
logical theory.

CHAPTER II

The Start of an Excavation

*

THE aim of the field archaeologist is to discover and to illustrate the course of human history; that really means that his task is a complicated one, and the unfortunate man is, in fact, serving two masters whose interests, though consistent, are not identical. On the one side he has to get his scientific record. As I said above, there is more to be learnt from the facts of discovery than from the actual things discovered, so that from this point of view the very finest object, when once it has yielded up all the historical evidence it can afford, has exhausted its interest and might almost as well not exist; thus, if the earthquake which in 1927 shook Crete had wiped out the Museum at Candia, with all its contents, instead of merely smashing one or two frescoes, it would have been a great artistic loss, but scientifically the damage would have been relatively small, because publication has put on permanent record the historical result of the excavations at Knossos, Phaistos, and the other Minoan sites.

On the other hand, the field worker is generally backed by an institution which is anxious to acquire specimens for Museum shelves – a perfectly good motive, because an appeal to the eye is the best way of awakening interest in a new form of knowledge – 'seeing is believing', and museums are a big factor in education. The archaeologist, therefore, has to be as careful about the preservation of objects as about the finding of them, and the demands on his time are thereby at least doubled. If he is working in a country like England this does not so much matter, for he can generally get in skilled help to deal with an emergency, but where an expedition has to be self-supporting one man cannot expect to be able to cope with all its needs, and there arises the question of the staff which he is to take with him.

The running of an expedition in the field involves a great deal beyond the actual dig. Pay-sheets have to be made out, correspondence written, accounts kept, the camp has to be housed and fed: if it is an excavation in which inscribed documents are found the excavator must know at least the gist of these, so that he may keep up to date with his discoveries and have as much light as possible to direct his course; surveys must be made of the site and plans drawn up of each building as it is found: even assuming that the head of the expedition can do each of these things, he cannot do them all, and so he must provide himself with an architect, and an epigraphist to deal with the inscriptions, and he will require at least one assistant for the general archaeological work; four or five people, all specialists in their several lines, are the minimum with which a big excavation can be run successfully. I must emphasize strongly one thing. All excavation is destruction. The archaeologist unearths a building, perhaps removing two or three later constructions in order to do so; its walls remain and can be seen or, if the wind-blown sand covers them again, they can be dug out a second time, but all the evidence given by stratification, by the position of objects, by traces of wood ash or by fallen brickwork, has gone, and can never be recovered; he digs out a grave and all that remains is a hole in the ground and a group of objects in a museum; any evidence he has failed to note has gone for ever, and unless his record is scientifically complete he has defrauded science, and had better not have dug at all. With this heavy responsibility he must be assured beforehand that he has a staff sufficient to do full justice to the work he would undertake.

Does the archaeologist, then, do no digging himself?

In some sites, especially in a country like England, excavation is often on a very small scale, employing only six or a dozen men, of whom some may be volunteers interested enough to be very careful and to need less supervision than the casual labourer; in that case the director of the work may well be one of the gang. When excavating a Late Celtic graveyard near Canterbury I could take my turn with pick and barrow and still lose nothing of what my five men were doing; but on a site like Ur work on so small a scale would produce no results at all. There a big gang has to be employed, and because the overhead expenses of travelling and so on are necessarily heavy and the season is short, and because funds for archaeological work are hard to raise and must be used to the best advantage, the most economical thing is to engage the largest number of workmen possible, the largest number, that

is, that can profitably be employed on the
particular site chosen for excavation and with
which the staff can adequately cope. This is no
fixed figure. If it is proposed to excavate temple
ruins, where there is a vast amount of earth to
be shifted and objects are likely to be few, a
staff of five may manage 300 men, provided that
they have good foremen to back them in the
actual supervising. Digging in the great cemetery at Ur, where the graves produced objects
in abundance, requiring much fine work and
elaborate note-taking, but lay deep down in the
soil and so were slow to come at, the same staff
was hard put to it to keep pace with 180 men;
had similar graves been found near the surface
our gang would have had to be halved. At Ur
the work of a big gang like this is organized as
follows. All the men are directly under the
orders of three trained and trusted Arab foremen, who are not Iraquis, but come from far
away in North Syria, whereas the workmen are
recruited from the neighbourhood. They are
divided up into small parties consisting of a pick-
man, a spade-man, and three or four basket-
men; of these the pick-man is selected for his
experience and his superior intelligence – he is
generally one who has been employed by us for

a number of years, and is not so old as to have grown stupid nor too young to exercise authority; he uses an army entrenching-tool (the best tool I know for excavating in Iraq) and is the head of his little gang; since he does the actual cutting-away of the soil it is he who discovers things, and it is up to him to see that he exposes them without damage. The second man, armed with a long-handled native spade, puts the loosened earth into the baskets, and if the pickman has missed anything the spade-man ought to see it: the basket-men are either the older fools or the young recruits, and their job is purely mechanical – they simply carry the full baskets to the light railway, tip the earth into the wagons and come back for more. As individuals, the basket-men count, perhaps, for less, but it must be remembered that on the distance which they have to go and on the pace at which they walk depends the whole progress – and the cost – of the excavation; the director has to see to it that the railhead is as close as possible to the dig, the foreman that there is no slacking on the road.

The Arab foreman is, next to the archaeologist himself, the most important person on the excavations, for on him depends the conduct of the whole gang of diggers. He not only makes them work – the foreman who sits on the ground and just yells 'Y'Allah, y'Allah,' is not doing his job, even though the men run in answer to his cry; he must be himself the most highly skilled man on the ground, so that he can teach the rest their business, and take over from them when anything is likely to overtax their powers – and that means that he must know the quality of each individual man, and must carry in his head exactly what each small gang is doing, so that he can visualize the difficulty almost before it arises; he must have that enthusiasm which inspires the workers to do their best, not merely because they are driven, but through a pride in their job; and he must be a diplomatist who can settle quarrels and keep the gang in a good temper. Such a man, when found, is a 'jewel of great price', and I suppose that there are few archaeologists who do not nurse the belief that their own particular foreman is the best of his race.

It is an almost universal rule that the excavator should pay 'baksheesh' to his men for the objects they find, over and above their wages. It might be argued that a workman, paid a fair wage, has no claim to an extra reward for what his work may produce, but in practice the 'baksheesh' system is essential. In the first place, the finding of an object does give you a certain feeling of possession, and that moral claim warrants compensation if you have to hand the object over to someone else; so the reward is primarily an insurance against theft, and generally it is reckoned at the sum which an agent for an antiquity-dealer might pay for the object were it stolen. Then, it is a direct encouragement to good work; for an object broken by the digger little or no reward is paid, so it is to his interest not only to keep his eyes open but to deal carefully with what he has seen – and where work has been carelessly done it is far less invidious for the archaeologist to withhold a reward than to cut from an earned wage. At Ur the gang of five or six men working together is the unit amongst which the 'baksheesh' is distributed; all are paid at a flat rate of wages but the pick-man, who finds most of the things, and has to do the delicate work, gets the lion's share of the reward, the spade-man rather more than half of that, and the basket-men only a small proportion; in every discovery made in their particular patch of ground all have a financial interest, and theft by any one of them would mean the defrauding of the rest, so that mutual suspicion (and the foreman sees to it that the gang is not composed of men likely to league together to steal) practically ensures our losing nothing. Naturally, a pick-man skilled above the average is likely to be put to work where good results may be expected, and therefore does better in 'baksheesh' than the rest; and since the system is extended to giving extra pay for good work as such, even where the finds may have little intrinsic value, all recognize that skill is at a premium, and by degrees they learn to appreciate it for its own sake. On an average season the 'baksheesh' bill may come to 15 per cent of the wages; it is not very much, but it has an effect which doubling the wages would never produce. The sporting element which it introduces into the unaccustomed routine of work has a special appeal for Arabs, who are gamblers by nature, but I have found it just as effective, I think, with Italian workmen, or English; and the fact that every unexpected stroke of good fortune means luck for them as well as satisfaction to the employer does create an astonishing amount of good will. At al 'Ubaid I had spent three weeks preparing to remove a copper statue of a bull, and at the last moment the whole thing collapsed in useless fragments of green decay; in the dinner-hour I overheard an Arab commiserating with one of the gang concerned on the presumably handsome 'baksheesh' which would have been forthcoming if the operation had succeeded and would now never be paid: 'To hell with the baksheesh,' retorted the other, and went on to declare that he would gladly have given a week's pay to have lifted safely what had cost so much time and trouble. Of course he would not have surrendered his pay had it come to the point, but that he could imagine himself doing so meant that he was genuinely keen on the success of the work. Very few men will not take pride in doing a job well, provided that it gets fair recognition, and our trained Arabs will take infinite pains in following up a brick wall, and cleaning the face of it so as to preserve its mud plaster intact, even though there is no hope of reward to be got from it – 'it is in the interest of science!' they say with resigned cheerfulness, knowing nothing of what science is; but they do not disguise their preference for the spot where objects may await discovery and 'baksheesh' abound.

The moment a pick-man sees anything of possible interest, the face of a mud-brick wall, the green of copper or bronze, a clay pot, or

simply a change in the character of the soil, he
has to report it to the nearest foreman who,
taking over the pick, satisfies himself as to what
is really there, and either tells the man to carry
on, giving him the necessary instructions, or
calls up one of the staff. Then the archaeologist,
who the moment before may have been writing
notes in a different part of the field, has to take
his turn with the pick, or more probably with a
knife, and may spend the next few hours
crouched in the same hole, in the same uncom-
fortable attitude, engrossed in the cleaning,
recording and safe removal of some one particular fragile object. Obviously the shifting of
dirt must be left to the workmen, and such
digging as the archaeologist has to undertake
himself probably involves very little hard
manual labour; but, all the same, quite a large
proportion of his time *is* spent in digging, and
there are few of the really good objects found at
Ur which were not excavated wholly or in large
part by the hands of the English staff. The
difficulty is to combine this necessary work of
detail with the supervision and recording of
what is going on in all the other parts of the
field; every now and then while excavating the
cemetery we have had to shift the men tempor-

arily to some other site where, in the upper levels, nothing requiring much supervision was likely to turn up, so that we ourselves might be free to concentrate on the salving of treasures which one or two small gangs had brought to light. About that sort of work I shall have more to say later on; here I have only brought it in to show how things are organized, and what is the division of labour; before describing how objects are dug up I should like to give some idea of how one starts to find them.

To begin with, there is the choice of a site. In the early days of archaeology this was simple enough; the great cities of the ancient world called for excavation and promised rich rewards; Athens, Troy, Babylon and Nineveh, Persian Susa and Egyptian Thebes or Memphis such were bound to produce treasures of art and history, and in a capital city the best artists would have been employed and the scribes would have been kept most busy. It is thanks to work done upon these first-class sites that we now know so much more of the history and achievements of the old empires than was known to our greatgrandfathers; not one of them has been exhausted, has yielded up all its secrets, but not one has failed to give us a detailed and a dramatic picture of a centre of ancient culture. But every addition to our knowledge has brought fresh problems, more far-reaching than the picture we have drawn. Thus excavations in Italy have illustrated the entire civilization of the Etruscans; work at Mycenae and at Tiryns has shown us the glorious state of the Achaean kings of whom Homer sang; but who the Etruscans and the Achaeans were and whence they came we have not found out, and no digging in Italy or Greece is likely to tell us; for the sources of a familiar civilization we may have to search far afield. And since we need an answer to such problems if we are to understand the old world as a whole, the wise archaeologist, planning a dig, will not let himself be spell-bound by a famous name. He will pass the outstanding questions in review and try to think where the solution of any one of them is most likely to be found, taking into account history and legend, geography, language and what he knows already about different cultures, and so he may be led to some district – a wide district perhaps – within which he must select the actual spot that seems to offer the best promise.

Supposing that an excavator, having done all this, has taken the field, has pitched his camp and has enrolled his men, and proposes to begin work on the site of some buried town where no digging has been done before and there is no previous knowledge to guide him, what is his first step to be?

First of all he will study surface indications. The site may be large, and he must choose a particular point of attack; very likely there may be something visible which may influence his choice. In Egypt the town mounds may cover many acres, but the position of a temple may be betrayed by fragments of stone, conspicuous where most buildings would have been of mud brick, or by patches of white dust, showing where a later generation has pulled out the buried stones and burnt them for lime. Where stone has been the usual building material the poorer houses would have walls of unshaped rubble only, and the presence of cut blocks holds out promise of something better. In Syria and Palestine a single isolated mound or *tell* generally represents the ancient city, and here its shape may give some inkling of what lies beneath – the higher lump at one end of a long ridge may be the fort or palace whose more solid walls have produced a greater mass of debris; a ring-mound broken by a gap at one point will stand for the ramparts and the town gate. In Mesopotamia, where a tangle of linked mounds may stretch for miles, the highest may be buildings deliberately raised on artificial platforms, such as the Ziggurat; or, in the majority of cases, they denote the quarters where human occupation has been most continuous, and the height is due to the repeated building of new houses over the ruins of the old. Very often the question can be solved by the broken pottery lying on the mound's surface. Thus at Warka or Erech, a very extensive site, one mound was obviously the Ziggurat or staged tower; another, littered with sherds of Parthian pottery, showed that its upper levels belonged to the very latest date at which the town had been inhabited; on the other hand a low bank on which one could pick up fragments of painted pottery and chips of flint or obsidian clearly represented part of the earliest settlement which either had never been built over in later times or, if it were, had been so denuded by wind and water that only the most primitive strata remained; on yet another mound quantities of Kassite potsherds, unmixed with any of later date, showed that building on that particular spot ceased soon after 1000 B.C. Provided, then, that he can date his pottery, the archaeologist has something to guide his choice, but in any case, whether he choose blindly or with reason, his method of action will probably be the same whatever his point of attack; he will begin by trenching.

A line is marked either right across a mound or from the top of it to well beyond its foot, and along this the gangs are placed with a measured square for each to work in; before the trench has got very deep, there are sure to appear fragments of walls running across it. Now the first point to settle is, whether these disconnected bits of walling are of the same date: if they are not, and in the case of a fairly high and steep mound they are pretty sure not to be, then one has to select the latest and concentrate on them; for to dig out simultaneously two buildings of different dates is to ask for trouble; it will become difficult, if not impossible, to assign objects to their right levels, and failing to get things in their true context we shall lose or confuse the chronological evidence, which is the main aim of archaeology. For the same reason trench-work ought to be stopped as soon as it has served its purpose by finding out the whereabouts of buildings, and the men should be switched off to follow the walls to right and left; it is wisest to work from the known to the unknown, and a wall is a good solid fact. In Egypt the task is generally an easy one, for Egyptian ruins are covered by sand and the sand falls readily away from the walls of mud brick or, more often, of hewn stone. It is far more difficult in moister soil to excavate mud brick buildings buried in the ruin of their own walls, for then the wall is of the same nature as the rubbish which lies against it, and it requires skill to distinguish between fallen and standing brickwork. I have known an archaeologist in Egypt, digging for the first time on a site of this sort, cut away every brick wall he encountered until of a building which when he started was standing six feet high there was left nothing but the thresholds of the doors, which happened to be of stone. Even stone walls are not always easy to follow; if built of rough rubble with mud for mortar they may have no true face left; the mortar may have oozed out, the stones slipped, until there is little to choose between the wall and the fallen rubble heaped against it; in the case of a wall faced with properly cut blocks, the face may have been carried off by a later generation as material for another building and there may remain only a rubble core which

scarcely looks like masonry at all. The greatest
test of an excavator's skill in this branch of his
work is when he has to deal with *terre pisée*
walls built not of bricks but of mere mud
rammed together – a primitive substitute for
reinforced concrete. Here there is no clean-cut
face to guide him, little difference of texture to
distinguish wall from heaped rubbish, and he
has to work almost as much by faith as by sight;
if, days later, when drying brings out the
nuances of colour, he can assure himself that he
has neither cut into his walls nor made false
walls by leaving what is mere earth standing in
the semblance of building, he will have good
reason to feel pleased with himself.

Even with good mud brick the work is not
always easy. At Warka (the ancient Erech) in
Mesopotamia the top of the Ziggurat mound
seemed to yield nothing but a uniform and level
mass of mud brickwork. The wind cleared away
the dust from its surface and the German
excavators noticed here and there straight white
lines, no wider than the thickness of a sheet of
notepaper, and following these up they discovered the ground-plan of a building; it was a
temple whose rooms had been nearly filled
with brickwork so as to make a raised platform

for a later structure, but the original walls had been whitewashed and when they were trimmed down the section of that thin coating distinguished the brickwork of the walls from that of the filling; but it required the eye of faith to see it. Similarly on a temple site at Atchana in North Syria where again rooms had been filled with well-laid bricks to make a platform but there was no whitewash to guide us, we found that if we scraped the surface of what seemed to be a featureless mass in the morning, after the night dews had moistened the brick, and then left it for a while, the ground-plan would appear, because the walls, with their deeper foundations, held the moisture longer and would still be dark in colour when the filling had dried to a lighter tint; but ten minutes later the ground-plan would fade away and uniform brickwork again confront the sun.

The finding of walls then may be easy or may be difficult, but it is the essential preliminary; only when there is something definite to go upon can the excavation follow rational lines.

While one gang goes ahead along each face of each wall, cutting a narrow trench for the purpose, others behind them go deeper to find floors if possible, and the rest are set to clear the

rooms as these appear. If there be a distinguish-
able floor, whether of brick or of beaten earth,
well and good, that should be for the moment
the depth-limit of the excavation; and if there
be none, the work should stop short where the
floor ought to be, that is, a little above the level
to which the wall foundations go down. The
sense of this is clear. Everything found above
floor level is contemporary with or later than
the building, everything found below the floor
is earlier; the man who stamped down that mud
to make a pavement for his house was sealing up
an archaeological stratum, and it behoves us to
profit by his good work, and not to confuse the
evidence which he has made so clear. Therefore,
the top building must be cleared first, its plan
drawn out, its contents duly noted, especially
the types of pottery found in it, and then, when
everything that can be learnt about it and from
it has been learnt, it must all be swept away, its
foundations rooted out, and the excavation of the
next level can begin.

In practice this is not always as simple as it
may sound. Sometimes a house has been ruined
and buried, but parts of its walls have been left
sticking up above ground, and the next builder
on the site has incorporated them in his new

house, so that the same walls really belong to two different periods. One house may have stood unchanged while its neighbour was rebuilt twice over, so that what is found in the rooms of the first corresponds in date to the contents of three distinct floor levels next door; or again, neighbouring houses of exactly the same date may, thanks to some accident of past building, stand at very different levels. All sorts of things such as these may confuse the issues, and it is the duty of the archaeologist to detect and make proper allowances for them, which he could never succeed in doing if he were not strict in his method and if that method were not controlled by common sense. We habitually speak of 'archaeological levels' and, describing our excavations, refer an object to 'Level VI' or 'Level IV' as evidence for its date; that implies careful measurement. But what is an 'archaeological level'? Sometimes a digger, determined to be on the right side, has started with a fixed datum line, such as the highest point on the surface of his site, and recorded the exact depth below that line at which every object was found – then the first ten inches, let us say, make up Level I, the next ten inches Level II, and so on; and this schematized section of the soil becomes his basis for chronology. There are occasions where the method is necessary and valuable, as, for instance, in making a section of a trench in an ancient earth-work; but for a town site it is worse than useless. Not only does it fail to take into account those accidents of building which I have just mentioned, but in the Middle East, at any rate, where town sites have resulted in the gradual formation of a *tell* or mound, the houses were necessarily stepped down the mound's sides so that those on the outskirts may be twenty feet or more below those in the centre; a horizontal line drawn through the middle of the mound fifteen feet below the top-surface datum-line so far from giving a single archaeological level might cut through half a dozen levels of which that in the middle would be centuries older than that on the circumference. Pure mathematics must here be controlled by observation and common sense, and the archaeological 'level' must correspond to historical fact.

To the general rule that one should begin at the top and go down layer by layer, there is one exception, justified only when the prime object of the work is not to clear buildings but to obtain certain definite information. It may be

essential to find out from the outset the
character of a mound, whether it represents a
long period or a single phase of history, and by
digging from the top we shall learn that only by
slow degrees; or our knowledge of the archaeology of a country may be so slight that we shall
have difficulty in assigning what we find in the
successive levels to the right points in the time-
sequence – we need a rule with which to
measure our discoveries. Then a different
method can be employed.

In Palestine a certain amount of scrappy
digging had been done, but no connected
history had been traced, and in particular very
little had been learnt about the pottery, and the
changing types of pottery vessels are the best
criterion of date than an archaeologist can have.
In 1890 Flinders Petrie went to dig at Lachish,
in south Palestine, an old Biblical city now
represented by a mound whose earth sides rose
steeply from the plain, and he simply drove a
trench into the steep side from top to bottom.
His pick-men, set one above the other at fixed
distances up the slope, had each to cut into it a
horizontal step; the objects, broken pottery and
so on, found by each gang were kept apart and
recorded separately. The division by gangs, was,

of course, artificial, not answering to anything in the stratification of the mound, but when the notes on each level were complete, and could be compared, the scientific results were perfectly clear. The types of pottery varied with the altitude; a shape common in the topmost five feet of soil might be rare in the next five, and entirely absent in the next; one could therefore put its starting-point at seven or eight feet from the summit of the mound and assume that it continued in fashion as long as the town was inhabited. A type might be found in fair quantities by one pick-man in his horizontal shaft and not by either of the men above and below him; confined to a narrow stratum, it must have been a short-lived type, and so the more valuable for dating because it allowed a smaller margin of error. There was no evidence for fixing exact dates because there were no written documents; but in a very short time Petrie was able to work out a schematic chart, in which every type of vessel found by him was assigned to its proper place in a historical sequence; for the first time Palestinian archaeology was provided with a sound chronological basis.

It might be thought that this was the natural

result of a very simple process, but actually there are few things more difficult than the working-out of a step-trench cut in the side of the mound. Petrie succeeded because he was an archaeological genius, but others have been less fortunate. I remember visiting the excavation of a lofty *tell* in India. On the very top they had cleared house ruins which were dated by coins and pottery to the Kushan period, and from the edge of the house site a deep cut had been made, with two or three steps, into the steep side of the mound, and here, just twenty-six feet below the houses, they had found groups of pottery and coins of precisely the same date as those on the house floors! The facts were indisputable, and they seemed to make nonsense of any particular time sequence; the excavators were at their wit's end. What had happened was that the workmen, digging in horizontally from the slope of the mound, had failed to notice (as they would almost inevitably fail) the slight difference in soil that marked the filling of ancient rubbish-pits which ran down into the ground from house-level; when therefore they came on the pots lying at the bottom there was nothing to connect them with the upper surface – or, at least, nothing very obvious. If the pits had contained pottery only one would have argued that the Kushan potters were very conservative and produced the same models for several centuries; but the presence of coins forced one to look for another explanation, and actually it was in one case possible to see, in the face of the cut soil, the two faint grey lines of discoloured earth that marked the sides of the rubbish-pit descending from house level to the cluster of pots at its bottom. The archaeologist's task is indeed beset with pitfalls.

CHAPTER III

Work on a Town Site

*

DIGGING on our town site began with a single long trench. Very soon this changed its appearance and spread to right and left, first with narrow trenches, then with rectangular clearings like so many shallow boxes separated by low walls. Now the ruins so long buried begin to take on shape and meaning, and the archaeologist is faced with fresh problems.

The first thing he will want to do is to establish the date and character of the building. Very often the date can be fixed only by the objects found between the walls, and then the exactness of the date will depend on how much is known of the antiquities, and particularly of the pottery, of the country. A Roman site in Britain can usually be brought within fairly narrow limits; even if no coins are found – and they are generally forthcoming – the local pottery is being studied with more and more definite results, and the red *terra sigillata* wares imported from the south of Gaul and from the Rhine factories give very accurate information, for we know within a few years when some of the potters were at work. In classical Greece the household wares are not properly classified, but even a fragment of a red- or black-figured vase can nearly always be dated to within thirty years, and though such precision is impossible in the pre-classical age and we have to be content with periods, these are being more closely defined, and when we can describe a house as 'Middle Minoan III' we are really saying all that it is essential to know. An exact chronology is of course the archaeologist's aim, but this can only be obtained by combining the results of many excavations and making use of such date-able objects as they may have produced. And the measure of success achieved is gratifying. When I wrote this book, in 1930, I was obliged to say that in Palestine and Syria the terms employed were even vaguer than those for the Greek world; the local pottery could still only be grouped into classes, such as 'Late Bronze Age', 'Early Iron Age', each of which covered several centuries; 'but even so', I added, 'we have a foundation on which the steps of a historic sequence can be built up'. Well, it has now been built. We now have a Middle Bronze Age divided into four sub-periods, a Late Bronze Age also of four sub-periods, giving, between the twentieth and the twelfth centuries, an average length for each sub-period of only a hundred years; and the Iron Age, from 1200 B.C. to 330 B.C., is divided into three phases.* This remarkable advance was made possible by the occurrence in Palestine and Syria of dateable Egyptian imports associated with local objects whose place in the sequence could be fixed on purely archaeological grounds.

In Mesopotamia a temple will often have in its walls a certain number of bricks on which there has been written or stamped an inscription giving the name of the temple, of the god to whom it was dedicated, and of the king by whose order or in whose honour it was put up; here then the archaeologist is given all the information he can expect. It may be that at different heights in the walls, or at different places, he may find brick inscriptions of different kings; this means that a later ruler has repaired the building of his predecessor, and with each

*On this see Professor Albright's Pelican book *The Archaeology of Palestine.*

name a new chapter can be added to the temple's history. Mesopotamian kings were very fond of recording their piety as temple-builders, and the inscription may appear not only on the bricks of the structure but also on clay cones hidden in the core of the wall, on the great stones which were set in brick boxes below floor level in the doorways to act as hinges for the doors, or again on copper figures and stone tablets which were placed as 'foundation-deposits' under the walls, just as today we may bury in a similar box coins of the realm and copies of newspapers. In Egyptian temples there will be inscriptions on the walls, and under the corner-stones foundation-deposits with the king's name inscribed on tablets of gold, silver, copper, stone, and wood, all the materials used in the construction of the building. Or there may be evidence of other kinds. At Carchemish, the Hittites, the Greeks and the Romans worked different quarries, and the quality of the stone in the walls served as a rough guide to dating until better evidence turned up. In Mesopotamia the shape and size of bricks varied fairly consistently at different periods, and by recording the dimensions of bricks whose age is fixed by inscriptions one obtains a tolerably reliable criterion for fixing the period of private houses and other buildings in which no inscribed bricks occur – in fact, after a time a mere glance enables one to make a pretty good guess at a wall's date. Absolute precision is too much to be hoped for – though recently at Ur an inscription did give us the actual year in which the temple we were excavating was founded – but in nearly every case the archaeologist ought to be able, by evidence of one kind or another, to define within reasonable limits the age of any building he digs up.

Then for the character of the building. An inscription may give the *fact* that it was a temple, but what we really want to know is, what kind of a temple or what kind of a house was it? Here comes in the importance of the plan. I remember hearing an antiquary of the old school declare that to dig out a ruin for the sake of its plan was a waste of money, because nobody understood or cared about plans – at any rate he didn't. Well, the business of the archaeologist is precisely to understand plans; he may have a professional architect to help him in the field work, but he must be something of an architect himself, and he will have just as much to do with the building on paper as with the scraps of brick or stone walling from which the paper plan is drawn up. The ground plan sums up what he has found of his building, and is the basis of what he will find out about it. One need not ask the layman to be enthusiastic about the plan of an ancient building, but the professional should, with the help of the plan, get information about the building which the layman will find of interest. We are digging up the past – not the existing ruin, but the temple or house which it once was; the ground-plan is the first and most obvious thing that we secure, but on it we have to build up, by the help of all the evidence we can find and all the knowledge we possess, the original edifice; that cannot always be done, but until it is done the archaeologist has not fully succeeded; and with this aim in view he must observe and record and weigh each fact, however minute and seemingly unimportant, that may help his task.

First of all, he has to decide what the plan is. Some walls may have been destroyed altogether and their line be but conjectural, though every effort must be made to support conjecture by evidence; I have known a Roman wall in Britain to be accurately planned when it had altogether ceased to exist. The Roman builder dug a trench for his foundations and put in it a bedding of clay for his stonework; here every stone had vanished, but a film of clay was traced for many yards through the loam of the meadow and gave the outline of the building. Or the walls may be too many, a senseless confusion, some being due to additions to or alterations of the original structure, and on paper these, which have their historical value all right, will have to be eliminated before the first builder's intentions become clear. And his main intention will be clear at once. Seldom could one mistake the ground-plan of a temple for that of a private house or of a fort. Passages, doorways, and rooms give the general arrangement, questions of lighting may show that one 'room' was necessarily an open courtyard; the thickness of walls may give a hint as to the existence of upper storeys; the bases of columns may be found, and a known canon of proportions between the length of a column and its diameter will show the building's height; a shaped stone or a specially moulded brick found loose in the ruins may prove the existence of arched doorways or vaulted roofs. In Crete, Sir Arthur Evans has actually rebuilt up to the second floor part of the Palace of Minos, though the walls he found were standing only a few courses of stone high;

basing his work partly on logical deductions from the plan, partly on minute observation of what was found in the course of the digging – the exact height and position of a threshold stone high up in the soil, the impression left in the earth by a wooden column whose substance had long since vanished – he has been able to bring before the eyes of the ordinary man (who certainly would not have cared for ground-plans!) the actual setting in which the Minoan kings lived their splendid lives. Let me, at the risk of egoism, give an extreme example of what a ground-plan may do in the way of recon-struction.

We were digging at Tell el-Amarna, in Egypt, the site of the city built by Akhenaton, the 'heretic king' who in the fourteenth century before Christ tried to impose a monotheistic religion on a people whose gods were legion. We visited a spot at the south end of the city where, inside a great walled enclosure, the sand, over a fairly large square area, was littered with fragments of worked stone. There were two battered column drums, one or two moderately sized building stones with carving in relief on two faces, but nearly all the rest were scraps and splinters from carved blocks which had been

hopelessly broken up; it was clear that the
heretic temple had later been used as a quarry,
its walls pulled down, their ornament defaced
and the material carried off to be employed
elsewhere. It did not look a promising site, but
I decided to excavate it on the chance that
something worth having might have been left.
Results were speedily forthcoming, and nothing
could have been more disappointing than they
seemed. Everything was on the surface; six
inches down, immediately beneath the stone-
masons' chippings, there extended a flat rectangular bed of cement, a foot or so thick, laid
down over the unstable desert sand as a foundation for the temple; there could be nothing
underneath it, all that was above it we had seen
before we began to dig. Of the temple not a
single stone remained in position, scarcely a
stone remained on the site.

On the cement foundation the limestone
blocks for wall and floor had been bedded in
mortar; when they were pulled up for removal
it generally happened that the mortar was left
adhering to the cement and bore on its upper
surface the impression of the stone; we could
count the stones which were not there, and even
see the toolmarks on them; looking at them

carefully I thought it might be possible to distinguish between the blocks which had been set in lines for the walls and those which had been the pavement of the rooms, so I told the workmen to sweep the whole surface clean with brooms. As Mr Newton, the architect of the party, and myself were examining the site, trying to decide whether it was worth while making a plan of the position of the blocks, we saw a peculiar thing.

Sometimes the mortar had come away with the stone, leaving the face of the cement clean, and here and there on the clean face there were faint red marks which carried on the lines of the mortar-impressions of what we supposed to be wall blocks. The explanation was obvious. When the cement foundation was dry the builders had worked out on it the architect's plan; a cord dipped in red paint had been stretched taut along the line of each proposed wall, the middle of it lifted and allowed to come slap down again on the cement, with the result that a red streak was left as straight as if ruled with a ruler; between two such lines the builder laid his wall-stones. We had no need to exercise our imagination, we had before us the actual plan drawn out by the Egyptian architect. Having transferred this to paper we could proceed to the next part of our task – to find out what the building was really like. The thickness of the walls varied considerably; a good many of the stone fragments bore reliefs on both sides and therefore must have gone right through from one face of a wall to the other, and they were not all of the same length. All such fragments were collected and measured, and assigned to one or other of the walls shown on the plan according as their length agreed with the wall's thickness.

Now the temple sculptors of Akhenaton's day had a very limited stock of subjects, and the scenes carved on the temple walls repeated each other monotonously; although we had only a few little scraps to represent each wall face, by identifying the subject and looking up parallels to it in better-preserved buildings it was easy to complete on paper the entire decoration of every wall. Two stone drums from columns of different sizes and types lay on the surface, and the plan showed that columns of two sizes had been employed; we could put our drums in their places, and since the proportions of Egyptian columns are pretty consistent, could decide their length, and therefore the height of the building. A few fragments of cornice took us up to the roof-line, a carved lintel completed the main door; we were able to restore accurately and in every detail a temple (incidentally a temple of a new type and therefore a valuable document for the history of Egyptian architecture) of which not one stone remained in position, and all but two or three had been smashed to atoms. One little detail gave us perhaps the greatest satisfaction of all. The flat cement foundation was considerably larger than the area of the building, and all round it, outside the walls, there were round holes about six inches across driven through the cement while it was still soft into the desert sand beneath; these puzzled us for a while, then, searching carefully, I found in one traces of decayed wood, and the mystery was solved. In the pictures we have of Egyptian temples there are always shown alongside them flagstaffs from which pennants were flown; here – and it is the only case in all Egypt where evidence of the sort has survived – we had the actual sockets for the flagstaffs, and in our drawing even that detail could be put in with measured accuracy.

I have described elsewhere the process of observation and deduction by which we were able to work out the original appearance of a private house at Ur in the time of Abraham. That is a case where, I think, everyone feels the genuine interest of the result, because it supplies a new and unexpected background to a familiar figure, and challenges us to re-cast our judgement of him; it is a very obvious case, because we had been accustomed to think of Abraham as a simple dweller in tents, and find him a possible occupant of a sophisticated brick house in a city; but there was more to it than that. A building style is neither an accident nor an arbitrary thing, but a natural growth answering to the conditions of life; an ancient building therefore is important, not merely as illustrating the history of architecture but as a setting for the lives of men and women, and as one of their chief forms of self-expression; if we do not know in what surroundings people moved and had their being we shall understand very little of their attitude towards life. To a large extent the influence of the building on the man is, of course, intangible; in so far as it crystallizes past traditions it is very real, but it is not directly translated into bricks and mortar. We can feel sure that the occupant of one of the Ur houses did inherit the spirit which had informed and grown out of centuries of splendid achievement in civilization and art, but we deduce that not from the mere existence of arched doorways and galleried courtyards but from the fact that such come in unbroken descent from the royal tombs of 1500 years before. The 'background' so essential to our understanding is something much more than the individual house; but it is none the less true that the actual ruins may give us, together with the architectural reconstruction, some particular feature which we can translate in terms of human thought.

By the time we had excavated a number of the private houses of Abraham's date it was clear that though no two were the same, yet there was a common idea underlying all of them; all were modifications of one general plan, and, therefore, each helped to explain the others. We could compare them and so identify the individual rooms in each; this was the kitchen, this the reception-room, this the lavatory, and so on; experience had taught the ancient architect exactly what type of house suited the habits of the people and the climate of southern Mesopotamia, and so well had he learnt his lesson that he set a standard for all time, and the modern Arab house of Baghdad is but a replica

77

of that in which Abraham might have lived. So one could argue backwards too, and use one's knowledge of the present-day Arab to explain the way of life of the inhabitant of the same land three or four thousand years ago. And there was more than this. At the back of virtually every house there was a rather long and narrow court-yard which always presented the same features; – one end had been open to the sky and under its paved floor there was a burial vault, while at the other end, below a pent-house roof, the pave-ment was raised and on it stood a low brick bench or table, a square brick altar in the corner, and in the back wall a fireplace for burning incense; when we could show that the ordinary householder of the time had in his house a special chapel set apart for domestic worship and that his forebears were buried there so that they too could take part in the family rites, then we had really learnt something about him, about his beliefs and thoughts, which, as a matter of fact, literature did not tell us and we should never have guessed.

Sometimes the picture of past life that a building gives is extraordinarily vivid. At el-Amarna we dug out a model village put up for the labourers who excavated the rock-cut tombs made in the desert hills for the aristocracy of the capital; it had been built all on one plan, and had been deserted when the court of Egypt moved back again to Thebes, and no more tomb-making was required. A square walled enclosure was entirely filled with rows of small houses divided by narrow streets; except for the foreman's quarters near the gate they were all monotonously alike, each with its kitchen-parlour in front, its bedrooms and cupboard behind, the very pattern of mechanically devised industrial dwellings. That alone was an interesting sidelight on the social conditions of the fourteenth century before Christ in Egypt, and supplemented well the information that the site of the capital itself gave us as to the palaces of the Government officials and the houses of the middle class. But it was the details which made the thing alive. Against one front door was a manger built up of mud and stone; in the side of it was contrived a square hole, across which was fixed a stick, and tied round this and trailing across the street was still the palm-fibre rope with which the donkey had been made fast more than 3000 years before. Inside the houses rough paintings on the mud walls hinted at the efforts of the individual workman to improve his surroundings or to express his piety; the charms and amulets picked up on the floor showed which of all the many gods of Egypt were most in favour with working men; scattered tools and implements told of the work of each, or of his pursuits in leisure hours. One house seemed to betray in really comic fashion the character of its owner. Whereas all its neighbours in the row opened on the street running to the east, this was the reverse way round, and opened on a back lane whose boundary was otherwise a blank wall. So striking an exception made us look more closely at the structure, and we found that the house as first built had been like all the rest, giving on the eastern street, but at some time or other it had been remodelled; the front parlour had been divided up into bedrooms, the old bedrooms thrown into a single room, and through its back wall a new front doorway cut. One could picture the owner who had quarrelled with his neighbours and hated the very sight of them, yet could not leave his house without running into one or another; being little better than a serf tied to his work, he could not move elsewhere to avoid their company; at last, in desperation, he changed not the position but the direction

PLATE I

Clearing Graves, Ur.

PLATE 2

Air photograph of the Roman town of Caistor, before excavation.
The lines of streets and buildings can be seen clearly.
(*Royal Air Force official – Crown Copyright reserved.*)

PLATE 3

The basket-men at work. A long climb to the waggons, Ur.

PLATE 4

Assessing the day's finds for 'baksheesh', Ur.

PLATE 5

Archaeological Strata, Ur.

(a) A pavement of Cyrus King of Persia, c. 525 B.C. (b) A pavement of Nebuchadnezzar, 600 B.C.
(c) Below the pavement, walls of Kurigalzu, 1400 B.C.

PLATE 6

Evidence of date. Temple walls at Ur with royal inscriptions on the bricks: (a) of Bur-Sin, 2220 B.C.; (b) of Kurigalzu, 1400 B.C.

PLATE 7

A 'foundation-deposit' at Ur.
(a) The box in the wall foundation. (b) The copper figure of King Rim-Sin, 1990 B.C.

PLATE 8

A foundation deposit at Ur. The stone tablet of King Rim-Sin.

PLATE 9

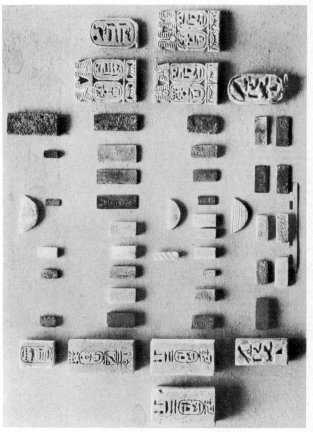

Plaques of various materials from the foundation-deposit of a Nubian King.

PLATE 10

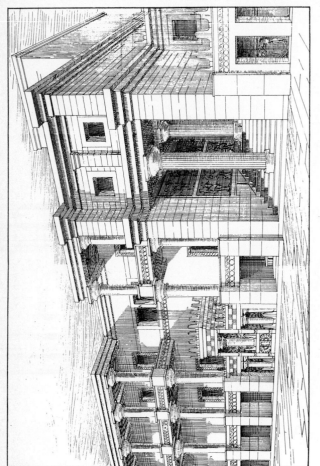

The Palace of Minos at Knossos. Reconstructed drawing of part of the West Palace facing on the central court. *By permission of Sir Arthur Evans.*

PLATE II

The Palace of Minos at Knossos. Restoration of
the actual building. (*a*) Room of the Priest-King.
(*b*) Stepped porch and central staircase.
By permission of Sir Arthur Evans.

PLATE 12

Plan of the 'model village' for workmen at el-Amarna.
By courtesy of the Egypt Exploration Society.

PLATE I 3

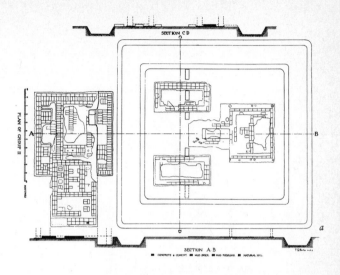

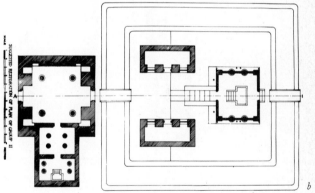

A temple at el-Amarna.

(*a*) The ground plan as found. (*b*) The ground plan as restored.

PLATE 14

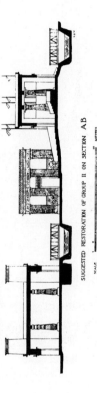

SUGGESTED RESTORATION OF GROUP II ON SECTION A·B

SCALE [⸺⸺⸺⸺⸺⸺⸺] METRES

A temple at el-Amarna. Suggested restoration of the ruined building
whose actual remains are shown in Pl. 13.

PLATE 15

A private chapel in a house at Ur showing the altar, the raised pavement of the chancel, and in the foreground the burial vault below the floor.

PLATE 16

Palace of Minos at Knossos. Reconstruction of the actual remains.
By permission of Sir Arthur Evans.

PLATE 17

The 'parlour' of a workman's house at el-Amarna. *By courtesy of the Egypt Exploration Society.*

PLATE 18

Inlaid gold coffin for viscera. Tomb of Tutankhamen.
By permission of the Griffith Institute, Oxford.

PLATE 19

The 'tomb-chapel' over the entrance of a tomb
at Karanog, with its brickwork undisturbed.
*By courtesy of the Trustees of the University
Museum, Philadelphia.*

PLATE 20

Part of a log coffin of the Bronze Age from a Scandinavian peat-bog
showing the body with all the garments preserved.

PLATE 21

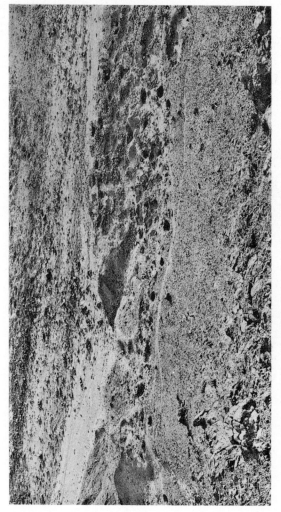

A pre-dynastic cemetery in Southern Egypt, showing the close-set grave hollows in the sand.
By courtesy of the Department of Antiquities, Egyptian Government.

PLATE 22

'Cleaned for photographing'. Two pre-dynastic Egyptian graves with skeletons and objects in position.

By courtesy of the Department of Antiquities, Egyptian Government.

PLATE 23

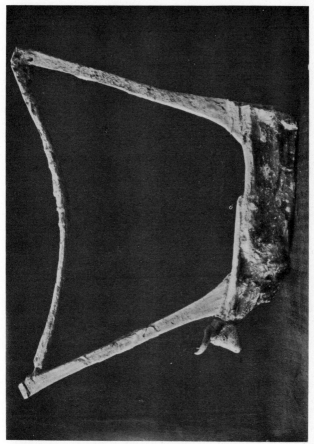

Plaster cast of a wooden harp with copper cow's head attached, Ur.

PLATE 24

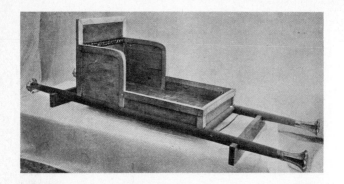

(a) The carrying-chair of Hetep-heres, restored.
(b) The arm-chair of Hetep-heres, restored.
By courtesy of Boston Museum of Fine Arts.

PLATE 25

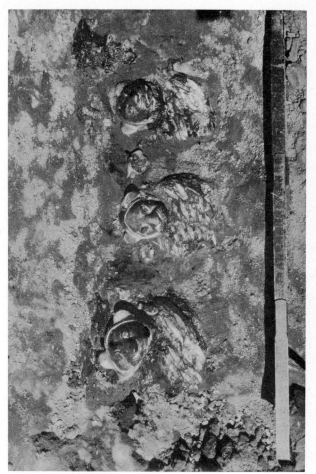

The gold lion masks of Shub-ad's sledge exposed in the ground.

PLATE 26

The body of Queen Shud-ad's sledge, restored.

PLATE 27

Removing a skeleton of the Flood period.
(*a*) The skeleton cleaned for photography.
(*b*) The skeleton, waxed and shrouded, being undercut so
that it may be turned over on to the padded board.

PLATE 28

Digging out tablets at Ur. They are at once packed in sand in tin boxes.

PLATE 29

Baking clay tablets at Ur. The tins are being put in a furnace heated by
vaporised oil from the reservoir on the house roof.

PLATE 30

Clay tablets from Ur.

(*a*) as found; (*b*) after being baked and cleaned.

PLATE 31

From the Pyramid tombs at Meroe. Objects showing the influence of old Egyptian art on the Merotitic.

By courtesy of the Boston Museum of Fine Arts.

PLATE 32

From the Pyramid tombs at Meroe. Imported objects of Greek origin.
By courtesy of the Boston Museum of Fine arts.

of his home, walled up the front door and made a new one at the back, and one can imagine the relief with which he made his escape into the empty lane, where there was no risk of meeting his enemies.

It might be objected that this is a chronicle of very small beer, and so it is; of course it does not matter one bit whether a few workmen lived on bad terms with each other thirty-three centuries ago; but that is not the point. The point is that ruins may preserve the record even of such trifles as this, supposing that one can read the evidence; if the archaeologist is duly careful in observing and recording his observations he may be rewarded with facts of history far more important. It is his business to find out not only what was the building he digs up and what it looked like before it was buried, but through what vicissitudes it passed, for these may reflect the fortunes of a family or even of a nation. Suppose that a thousand years from now the history of England was forgotten, London a buried ruin, and some lucky excavator chanced on the site of Westminster Abbey; with what remained of its structure and its monuments he could re-write whole chapters of the past and recall half of the great names and great events of English history. The archaeologist cannot hope for such good fortune as that, but from the ruins of quite an ordinary building he may learn a great deal, the interest of which extends beyond the mere fabric which he has discovered; he can link up the dumb witness of bricks and mortar and the odds and ends of jetsam with the life of the people. This is so essential a part of the archaeologist's task that an instance of its working may well be given at length.

The temple of the Moon goddess at Ur was originally built in mud brick by Bur-Sin, king of Ur, about 2100 B.C.; a century later it was rebuilt in burnt brick; some time afterwards it was destroyed by fire. That is the barest statement of the facts.

Bur-Sin's building was extremely solid, and might have lasted very much longer than it did; that it so soon had to be restored from floor level upwards must have been due to its destruction by the Elamites, who brought Bur-Sin's dynasty to an end, and sacked the city of Ur. The new walls contain burnt bricks stamped with the inscription of the second founder; this was Enannatum, a priestess, the daughter of the last king of Isin. After the Elamite invasion the overlordship of Mesopotamia passed from Ur to a line of kings who made the city of Isin the capital of the country, and Ur ranked as subject to them; it was favoured, in that the king's daughter took office as priestess there, and it was rich, insomuch that the ruined temple could be rebuilt on more costly lines than in the old days; we may conclude that Ur was passing through a phase of prosperous mediocrity. But Enannatum dedicates her building 'for the life' not of her royal father but of the king of another city, Larsa, who was her father's rival, and eventually wrested from him the overlordship of the country, founding a new dynasty of Mesopotamian kings. If the priestess thus shifts her loyalty while still boasting of her royal birth, we must suppose that the ascendancy of Larsa over Isin was gained by slow and more or less peaceful means; certainly it implies that Ur submitted with a good grace to the change of masters and continued in comfort. In the ruins there were found scattered clay tablets whose written dates mentioned virtually all the kings of Larsa in succession – business documents which spoke of a quiet life. But in the courtyard, on and around a solid base of brickwork, there was a litter of chips of black stone, fragments of a large monument bearing an inscription in two languages,

the Sumerian tongue of the south country and
the Semitic speech of Babylon and the north;
it had been a monument set up by and recording
the exploits of Hammurabi, the great conqueror
and law-giver (identical, as we believe, with that
Emraphel whose raiders Abraham defeated by
the Dead Sea). Hammurabi conquered Larsa
and won for Babylon the suzerainty of the whole
land; Ur submitted, and in this temple the
victor set up his war memorial. It had been
broken to atoms. Inside the temple the brick
pavement was covered with a thick layer of
charred wood and ashes; mixed with these were
hundreds of fragments of stone vases, some of
them bearing the dedications of kings already
ancient in Hammurabi's time, broken statues
and more tablets from the temple archives; the
temple had been sacked as well as burnt. The
dates on the new series of tablets took us down
through Hammurabi's reign, and up to the
eleventh year of the reign of his son, and then
they stopped short. Now the eleventh year was
called 'that in which the south country rebelled'
and the twelfth year 'that in which the King
destroyed the walls of Ur'. Those two phrases
tell us all that we know of contemporary history;
now put them side by side with the archaeo-

logical evidence and the story is plain. Ur had submitted quietly to Hammurabi, but joined in, if it did not lead, the rebellion against his son, and its citizens signalized their revolt by defacing the war-memorial of Babylon. Within a few months, before the litter of stone which symbolized independence had been cleared away from the Moon goddess's court, the northern troops had stormed the walls of Ur and, not content with dismantling its defences, had sacked its shrines, breaking into the treasuries and looting the precious metal, while they smashed on the pavements what was not worth carrying away, and had finished by setting fire to the temple and to all the quarter in which it stood. Not only could we win from the ruins a detailed and a dated account of the building's foundation and destruction, but we could see in it an epitome of the town's history over the space of 300 years.

I have chosen this instance chiefly because here the main facts were already known; the archaeological results of the dig had to be worked out independently, and then brought into relation with the records, and you can see how at every point they could be checked by external evidence and proved correct. Very often there is no previously recorded history, and the archaeologist is thrown back on his own resources; his deductions will not necessarily be beyond dispute, but I hope that I have shown that if they are logically based on the evidence they have every chance of being good history.

Suppose that he is digging into a mound where the remains of buildings lie one above the other in more or less definite strata, but all belong to a period or to a culture of which there is no written record, what sort of evidence is he going to find? That there should be material to illustrate the life of a forgotten people we may grant, but how can he arrive at historical events, at the sort of things that ancient chronicles might have told us?

Here comparative archaeology must come into play. Suppose that his lowest strata belong to the neolithic age, and yield little in the way of objects other than stone implements and sherds of rough, hand-made pottery; even so there are probably affinities with other sites, and he can decide to what branch of culture the earliest inhabitants must be assigned.

As the levels rise stone will give place to metal. It may be that the copper tools and weapons appear quite suddenly in a certain stratum, yet in forms that seem well established, the work not of a beginner but of a craftsman experienced in the use of metal; we look elsewhere and in some other country find the same forms of weapons and tools, but there their evolution can be traced from something simpler, perhaps from stone originals; then it is manifest that on our site they are not local products but imports from abroad. Perhaps while the revolutionary change from stone to metal takes place the pottery shows a perfectly uniform development; pottery-making is essentially a local industry, and if that is unaffected we can argue that the population did not change, and that the introduction of metal was due to peaceful penetration or trade. But suppose the excavator comes upon a 'burnt stratum'. A patch of ashes may result from mere accident and mean nothing; ashes spread over the greater part of a site and accompanied with the marks of burning on walls tells of the destruction of the town. Suppose now that in the stratum above the ashes there appear new forms of pottery having no kinship with what has gone before; this implies foreign influence, and, taken in conjunction with the evidence of destruction, points to foreign conquest, and if the new pottery can be traced the identity of the conquerors can be established. Instead of the ashes of a fire there may be a layer of wind-blown sand, or a bed of mud finely stratified as successive rain-storms have brought down dust and decaying brick to fill up the hollows where the water lay; these tell of the desertion of a site, and may introduce a change of inhabitants. In the *tells*, or mounds, of southern Palestine, the early Bronze Age settlements with their rough walls and native pottery give place to strata where more solid walls and new types of weapons, glazed scarabs and beads mark the Egyptian conquest of Syria. Higher up again the sudden appearance of iron weapons and of a very distinctive painted pottery unlike anything known in the country before, but closely akin to wares found in Asia Minor, bears witness to the invasion of the Philistines; we think of Goliath, with his iron armour, and of the Chalybes whom Homer had heard tell of as an Asia Minor race, who got their name as being the first workers in iron.

Sometimes the link is there but its meaning has to be argued out. In Egypt at the time of the First Dynasty, about 3150 B.C., we find cylinder seals used, little engraved stone or shell cylinders which were rolled on clay to make the sign-

manual of the owner; precisely similar seals were
in use in Mesopotamia. The cylinder seal is a
peculiar type not likely to be invented independently in two different countries; which country
then owed it to the other? In Egypt the cylinder
seal appears suddenly, and before very long goes
out of fashion; in Mesopotamia it is the standard
pattern for more than 2000 years. In Mesopotamia the natural and traditional writing-
material is clay, which takes a seal-impression
well; in Egypt it is paper, papyrus, on which
you could not roll out an impression at all, and
paper-using people would never invent the
cylinder seal. Clearly, then, these seals are at
home in Mesopotamia, and the Egyptians owed
them, directly or indirectly, to the Euphrates
valley.

Of course, comparative archaeology has its
dangers; one has to be sure of one's ground,
and superficial resemblances may be utterly
misleading. I remember a book which was
meant to prove the Asiatic origin of Central
American culture, and the main argument
adduced was a stone carving on a Maya site
representing an elephant with his *mahout*, a
subject which could only have come from India.
Unfortunately the author had relied upon a

drawing made by a French artist, *not* an archaeologist, who had done his best to make sense of a carving high above his head on the corner of a sculptured stone monolith, and the elephant and the *mahout* holding his goad were in his sketch unmistakable; but a photograph of the actual stone showed, equally plainly, a toucan, eminently an American bird, surrounded by demons. Very false conclusions have been arrived at by scholars who have compared the early painted pottery of different countries and, painstakingly analysing the designs into their simplest elements, have shown that these are identical and so have triumphantly claimed for the various wares a common origin. But the truth of the case is that those elements of design are necessarily simple and their possible range is very small – circles, squares, triangles, and wavy lines, they are the basis of all design. What matters is, first – how they are elaborated and combined into patterns, and second – how they are applied to the pot, for the primitive potter is not concerned with inventing a design as such, he is producing a painted pot, and the shape of the vessel and the part of it to which his decoration is applied are just as much a part of the 'design' as are his painted lines. We are dealing with the products of human handicraft, and a purely abstract analysis which neglects the human element is bound to be wrong. Again, we may be misled by too confident an assumption of knowledge. At a great many sites in Palestine, Syria and Asia Minor there has been found painted pottery of a sort long familiar to archaeologists as the ware characteristic of Cyprus in the Bronze Age. When therefore it occurred in excavations on the mainland it was regarded as proof of commercial relations between the mainland site and Cyprus, and since the chronology of the island was reasonably well established this 'imported' Cypriot pottery was unhesitatingly used as evidence for date. We found vast quantities of the ware at Atchana in the Turkish Hatay and I was quite prepared to accept the conventional view; but at Atchana we had independent dating evidence and after a time this evidence convinced us that while in the upper levels in which it was found it was indeed contemporary with what was found in Cyprus, examples of it coming from lower levels were a hundred and fifty years older than the earliest known in the island. Finally it became clear that this 'Cypriot' pottery was not by origin Cypriot at all but an import from Asia Minor which became so popular in the island that it drove all the old native wares off the market; when it occurred in Palestine or Syria it was again an import, but there it could not be dated by Cypriot chronology and is not necessarily a link with Cyprus at all.

Sometimes the link is by no means obvious. One winter at Ur we found deep under the royal cemetery, and quite distinct from it, a series of graves of a sort we had never seen before. The attitude of the body was unparalleled in later times, the pottery forms and the shapes of the stone vases were new to us, and the burials were marked by the presence of tumblers made of lead, a metal scarcely ever used in the royal cemetery. Now some years ago, at a place called Jamdat Nasr, nearly 200 miles away to the north, there were found remarkable clay vases with designs painted in red, black, and buff, and with them clay tablets inscribed with the oldest writing known in Mesopotamia, writing not by conventional signs but by pictures. Recently we had found in a deep pit at Ur fragments of this painted ware, and with them a few bits of plain red pottery of a sort not reported from Jamdat Nasr and not otherwise known at Ur. In one of our new graves that winter there was a red pot.

Of course I had already my ideas as to the date of Jamdat Nasr, and as to the date of the graves, and they seemed to me to agree; but the red pot was further evidence. I stated in my report that though no fragment of Jamdat Nasr painted pottery and no scrap of Jamdat Nasr picture writing had been found in or anywhere near the graves, yet these were certainly of Jamdat Nasr date. When we were back in London we started to clean a pot from one of these graves which was so thickly encrusted with earth and salts that nothing of its surface was visible; as the dirt came off there appeared the geometrical patterns painted in black, red, and buff on the authentic Jamdat Nasr ware. The link was an indirect one, but the comparative method was justified in its results.

I have talked of the 'date' of Jamdat Nasr; it was a loose expression and perhaps I ought to retract it, certainly not to let it pass without a warning. The archaeologist can re-create a great deal of human history; he can bear witness to its vicissitudes, trace the progress of civilization, define the life of a city or of a nation by periods arranged in true historical sequence; but in the absence of written records he cannot fix dates. We are always being asked 'When did such and such an event happen?' We may know very well at what point in a sequence it occurred, but we cannot express our answer in terms of years. There is no empirical method of attaining such knowledge. The stratification of the soil on an ancient site does not go by mathematical progression; if each of the first three feet represents a hundred years it does not follow that ten feet equal a thousand; they may stand for 400 or 3000 years. The archaeologist may for his convenience talk in round numbers, but he is not really thinking in numbers at all, and if asked for dates he can only reply that he does not know. As we pass back, then, from history, which depends largely on written records, to pre-history, the archaeologist's peculiar sphere, we have to accept periods instead of dates, and racial movements instead of the exploits of individuals; it is an impressionist picture painted with a broader brush, but it is not necessarily less true.

Written history tells us nothing about Britain before 55 B.C., and then deals only with the invasion of an island which we should suppose to have been inhabited by barbarous savages. Archaeology can tell us of British kings in the south and east civilized enough to mint their own coins with dies modelled after the famous gold pieces of Macedon; by imports from the iron-workings of Hallstatt in Hungary, by the forms of bronze tools and weapons, by clay beaker cups, by megalithic monuments, it can trace trade relations with the Continent and the invasions of Continental tribes, can follow the shifting of the population as the older elements gave ground before the new-comers, can re-create in broad lines the beginnings of England. Nearly all that we know of Roman Britain, its topography, its economic conditions, the life of its people and the organization of government, is due to excavation; history has supplied little more than the skeleton. In *Puck of Pook's Hill* Kipling gives a picture of the Roman Wall as vivid as if he were describing life on the North-West frontier of India in the nineteenth century; the Roman writers have nothing to say about the great rampart which defended Britain from the Picts, nothing about the hot springs of Bath, or the villas of the Isle of Wight, but for every detail Kipling could quote the authority of the spade.

Here somebody might raise an objection. If, where periods have to serve instead of dates, archaeology can still present so complete a picture, why was it stated a little while back that the archaeologist's aim is an exact chronology? Really there is here no contradiction. From the stratified remains on your site you may work out the whole sequence of the development of an ancient community and describe its character in each successive phase; it is a valuable piece of work. But that community did not exist in a vacuum, it was one unit in a world of men; and if you are asked, what was the rest of the world doing? at any one stage of its advance was your community blazing a new trail for mankind or was it left behind in a backwater by more cultured nations? you cannot answer because you don't know the date of that stage. Someone in your community brings in a new technique; but the same technique is practised in some other land; which really invented it, and which learnt it from the other? Unless you can date the invention in each country you cannot rightly give credit to either. The value of an exact chronology is that it brings your community into its proper relation with the world of which it was a part, so that the isolated record takes its place in the ordered history of man.

CHAPTER IV

Grave-Digging

*

I HAVE dealt hitherto with the excavation of buildings and what one can hope to learn from them, and I have, I trust, made it clear that most of the information which we thus acquire is based either on the actual fabric and ground-plan, or upon contents which in themselves may have but little value. In the ruins of a temple there may, with luck, be statues and inscriptions, in a private house such odds and ends as the last inhabitants did not trouble to carry off; but if you go into a museum and look at the antiquities collected there, you can be sure that the vast bulk of them were found not in buildings, but in graves.

All over the world, and at most periods in the history of each part of it, a belief in some kind of life after death has induced man to place in the graves of his dead things which may minister to the needs of another world; conversely, from the fact that a grave contains such objects, we can deduce that there prevailed a belief in a future life. I am not speaking of such very personal things as decency would naturally leave to the corpse, the pin that fastens cloak or winding-sheet, the ring on the finger, the amulet worn in life about the neck, nor again of such things as might be considered mere offerings to the memory of the dead, the sword by the warrior's hand, the toy with which the child played and none other must play, the wreaths of flowers which are our modern expression of sad respect. 'Grave furniture', to use an archaeological phrase, is something far more definite than this, and answers to far more definite ideas.

The Greek placed on the dead man's mouth a coin to pay Charon his fare for ferrying him across the river of Death. The Egyptian might take with him a copy of the Book of the Dead to prompt his memory so that he might give the right answers to the gods or demons who held the gates of the under-world and cross-examined all who would pass through. In Mesopotamia vessels of food and drink provide sustenance for the long journey which the dead must undertake, and during one period these vessels are stacked on a boat made of bitumen, implying that the journey must be made by water. But the journey is not everything, there is the whole life of the next world, and because it is difficult to imagine life otherwise than in terms of that which we know, it is assumed that man's occupations and needs hereafter will be very similar to what they have been in the past – the next world is a continuation of this. Whatever, therefore, a man used and required in his lifetime he will use and require after death. The woman takes her spindle, her needle, her mirror and her cosmetics, the jeweller his balance and weights, the carpenter his saw and chisels, the soldier his weapons of war. The king must be provided with a goodly sample of his pomp on earth: the viking leader is laid in his barrow on the deck of his beaked galley with all his gear about him; the Sumerian king has not only his treasure of gold and silver, alabaster, lapis, and bronze, but the bodies of his slaughtered court to bear him company and to minister to him in his new sphere of royalty; the Pharaoh, in the rock-hewn labyrinth of his tomb, had such provision for his splendour that the grave of Tutankhamen, one of the most insignificant of Egypt's rulers, found intact, has astonished the whole world with its riches. It is not surprising, then, that the archaeologist derives much of his material from the cemeteries of the old world, and that what he there finds illustrates not only the beliefs and burial-customs of the past, but also its everyday life.

Yet it must not be supposed that such a wealth of objects and information is easy to come by – that it lies in the ground just waiting for the 'Open Sesame' of the spade; only too often the excavation of an ancient cemetery is a most disappointing task.

Legend says that when St Patrick landed in Ireland one of the natives showed him a round-topped tumulus or mound and explained that inside it was the body of a king lying on gold heaped half a spear's length high. The saint promptly dug into the grave and found the gold, and in gratitude transferred from Purgatory to Paradise the soul of the old pagan who had thus provided funds for the propagation of the Faith. The fact that so much gold was buried in the tomb could not have been hid, and would not be forgotten; when a new race enters the land, or a new religion takes the place of the old, the superstitious fears which guarded the treasure lose their force and the tomb is looted. Even without such a change, avarice may prove stronger than piety. At Ur we can trace in the soil of the great cemetery the tunnels by which thieves made their way down underground to the royal tombs when the whereabouts of these were still definitely known, perhaps marked by chapels built over them on the ground surface. Of all the tombs of the Pharaohs in the Valley of the Kings at Thebes only one, that of Tutankhamen, was overlooked by the robbers. And the robbers were early at work. We actually possess the written minutes of a Commission which was appointed by the Pharaohs of the twentieth Dynasty to inquire into the wholesale plundering of those very tombs in the Theban Valley. Nor was such plundering confined to the wealth of kings. Of the ordinary rock-cut tombs of Egypt 99 per cent have been looted in antiquity and most of the remainder have been spared only because it was known that their contents were not worth the risk and labour of breaking into them; from the plundered graves the modern archaeologist may hope to recover objects which the old thieves overlooked or deliberately discarded; in the rare cases where he comes upon a tomb intact he cannot help indulging in high hopes, but sober experience warns him beforehand that in all probability there is little to reward him there. At a place called Karano'g, in South Egypt, I excavated a large cemetery dating to the beginning of the Christian era, and secured a wonderful collection of objects belonging to the then scarcely known Meroitic civilization, but amongst them all not one thing in precious metal. The graves were chamber-tombs cut in the firm Nile mud, with a sloped passage leading down to the doorway. In nearly every case the brick wall that blocked the door was intact; but at the back of the grave there had been a pit, down which libations for the dead were poured, and the robbers had simply got into the pit and burrowed a hole through into the chamber, a hole, perhaps, only big enough for a man to put his arm through. But that small hole was enough; the thief knew exactly where each object of intrinsic value had been placed. We, entering by the door, would find everything apparently undisturbed; the painted clay vases, the bronze bowls, the glass bottles, and toilet-box of wood inlaid with ivory were all in their places, the body stretched out orderly and in peace. Then one would see, beyond the head, the jagged hole in the wall of grey mud; two or three fallen beads by the neck would show how the string had been snapped and the necklace snatched away; the right arm might have been bent up and back and a finger torn off for the sake of a gold ring; and if there had been any other object of precious metal (and its place then would surely have been near the head) it, too, had gone and left no trace. All the thefts had been committed by men who knew precisely where their booty was, and one can imagine that the sexton of the graveyard took careful notes of every funeral and made a very handsome profit on his inside information.

On the whole, therefore, whether it be a question of the Bronze Age tumuli of the British Isles, of Egypt's rock-cut shaft and gallery tombs, of the earth graves of Mesopotamia, or the bee-hive tombs of Mycenaean Greece, the archaeologist must content himself with the leavings of older and less scientific plunderers, and will rarely find the treasure-house untouched.

But this is not all; apart from robbery there is the question of soil and circumstance.

In an Egyptian tomb cut in the living rock, absolutely dry and protected from the air by the sand which seals it almost hermetically, there is little to bring about decay. Woodwork

may be shrunk and warped, will have lost much
of its substance and be light and brittle, but it
is generally still there, and the bedsteads and
the chests, the wooden coffin and the figures
carved in wood have suffered small damage
from the passage of 3000 years; even cloth
preserves its nature, and the linen sheets of the
bride's trousseau buried with her are still soft
and strong, though yellowed by age, and could
almost be used today; while such things as
copper and bronze have undergone only surface
change. From the peat bogs of Denmark the
digger may unearth a coffin made of a hollow
tree-trunk, and find in it the body of some old
Bronze Age warrior, with his clothes of wool
and leather discoloured but uncorrupted. In
the graveyard of Ur, where, perhaps, only a
layer of matting protected the dead man and
his furniture from the damp and salt-laden soil,
all these fragile things decay; of wood there is
left but a patterned stain on the smooth face of
earth, a paper-thin film grained in white and
grey which can be seen and photographed but
which a breath will make to vanish; copper and
bronze may be reduced to a shapeless mass of
green corrosion, and silver to a purplish powder;
even the bones may have mouldered away, leav-

ing only the teeth to show that here was a man; it is an irony of nature that our teeth, which decay so painfully while we live, stop decaying at our death, and outlast all the rest of us! Where an ancient people practised cremation instead of interment there may be even less to find, for the personal ornaments which survive on a buried body were often burnt with it. In the richest cremation-grave we ever discovered at Carchemish, that of a prince, apparently, who may have died in about the year 604 B.C., we found in the urn, mixed with the blue and grey splinters of calcined bone, a quantity of gold ornaments which must have adorned the dead man's dress; if they had not been actually flung upon the pyre they must at least have been put in the urn while the gathered ashes were still hot, for half of the delicate work, a unique treasure of archaeology, had melted and run into shapeless drops of yellow metal. It is true that a cemetery will, as a rule, yield far more objects than will the buildings of a town, but, at the same time, we can hope to recover only a small proportion of what the mourners put into the graves.

The method of digging graves must, of course, vary with the nature of the graves themselves.

In Egypt a pre-dynastic graveyard consisted of shallow pits or troughs dug into the sand along the desert's edge; scrape away the modern surface of wind-blown sand and the circles of greyer filling will betray the position of every burial – at least to eyes trained to see. For shaft-graves, again, the sand and gravel must be scraped away, and the rock exposed into which the square pit was hewn, and its outlines will show up at once, and then it is merely a matter of clearing out the rubbish from the pit until, thirty or fifty or perhaps a hundred feet down, the door is reached which leads into the tomb chamber. I have already explained how the Hittite graveyard at Yunus, near Carchemish, was located by the deep-rooted weeds growing in clumps out of the hard gravel soil; there we could dig where surface indications gave away the whereabouts of graves underground. At Ur we must needs dig uniformly over a wide area, for there are no surface signs, and the graves go down one under the other to varying depths, so that today a great excavation nearly eighty yards long and sixty wide and as much as forty feet deep alone testifies to the 1800 graves which our notes record.

Coming to the actual work, the first principle

of grave-digging is that nothing be moved. The excavator's record in notes, photographs, and drawings must show every object in its original place. This may sound rather like morbid curiosity, or like mere method run to extremes for its own sake, but it is not; perhaps very little information will result from this careful detail, but a great deal *may*, and where everything has to be learnt the excavator cannot afford to neglect any evidence whatever from which knowledge may afterwards be gained, even though it has no obvious bearing at the time. So he will plot in the position of the grave, measure its depth in the soil, and then proceed to deal with its contents.

To keep objects in their original place is not always easy. Their condition is often such that you can scarcely touch either them or the earth round them without a disaster. In the case of burials set close together in the soil, where even the outline of the individual grave is difficult to define, one does not always know to which grave a given object may belong; an outlying vase, for instance, discovered while one grave is being dug, may prove to be part of the furniture of another not yet found; and though a wrong attribution might not seem so very important a mistake, it does matter, not for sentimental reasons, but because it might upset a whole system of chronology. Then, again, it is possible that some offerings were put into the grave-shaft while it was being filled up with earth, and so lie not on the same level as the grave but right above it; unless these are very carefully noted, their association with the grave will be lost, and, incidentally, the evidence for that particular custom will also pass unnoticed. So one tries to recognize as soon as possible the grave's existence, and from that moment begins specially careful work.

One of our richest graves at Ur, that which contained the famous golden helmet, was located by the discovery of a copper spear-head sticking point upwards in the earth. The soil was cleared from round it, and there came to light a length of thin gold tube which adorned the top of the shaft; below this there was a hole in the ground left by the wooden shaft itself when it turned to dust. We followed the hole downwards, and it led us to the grave, against the corner of which it had been leaning when the earth was thrown back into the pit; with this forewarning we were able to trace the entire outline of the grave before we started to lay bare its contents, and so could record in order all the offerings heaped and crowded round the coffin. In another case, a simple hole in the ground was found, and then a second; something unusual about their shape seemed to call for special treatment, and accordingly plaster-of-paris was poured in to fill up the void which decaying wood had left: the result was a complete plaster cast of a harp whose substance had long since vanished (except for the copper bull's head and the shell plaque which decorated the front end of it and were later found sticking to the plaster), and thus the first hint that we had of a grave's presence also enabled us to preserve the best object in it before we knew what it was – in fact, before we really knew that the grave was there. One has to look out for all such little things; for the thin powdery white streak which represents the matting that once lined the pit, for the holes in the soil where once were the upright wooden ribs of a wicker coffin, for the rim of a tall clay vase standing in the grave and not crushed flat by the earth's weight; on encountering any such thing the well-trained Arab pick-man will stop his work and report to the foreman the likelihood of a grave; then the pick will give place to the knife for careful work, and the excavator will get out his note-books and his measures.

The clearing of a grave may be a long job. The mere removal of the earth so that the objects stand out well enough to make a good distinct photograph will require time and patience, especially as none of them may be moved in the process, and many may be very delicate or actually broken into pieces which only the earth holds together more or less in shape. In the case of the simplest grave the excavator's notes will give the attitude and direction of the body – sometimes a very important point, for there has often existed, as there exists today, a ritual determining such things, and that ritual may decide a period, a race, a religious belief; then there will be a drawing, or notes, giving the position of all the objects, including such details as, for instance, the order in which beads of various sorts were strung around the neck or arm; obviously a necklace is much more interesting if it is re-strung in its original order, and tells us more about the fashions of dress than would an arbitrary arrangement of beads collected promiscuously from the grave; but to obtain that the excavator may spend painful hours stooping or lying over the body as he cuts and blows away the earth so delicately as to leave the loose beads undisturbed. Then there will be measurements and measured drawings of the individual objects, and each of these will be marked with a number corresponding to that in his notes, so that subsequently the entire tomb-group can be reconstituted for exhibition or for study. But the labour required for noting an ordinary grave may be enormously increased when there are delicate objects in bad condition, or where there is material for reconstructing an object which itself is broken or decayed; few people, looking at such an object in the glass case of a museum, realize what it cost to get it there.

A fine example of the patience which goes to the saving of an antiquity is given by the tomb of Queen Hetep-heres, found by Dr Reisner close to the Great Pyramid at Gizeh. In a walled-up recess behind the rock-cut chamber in which stood the empty stone coffin of the mother of King Khephren, the Pyramid builder, there lay a mass of decayed and powdered wood and bits of gold plate, and scattered over the floor were tiny figures cut in gold, hieroglyphs which had been inlaid in the wood and had fallen out as that crumbled to dust. Had these just been gathered up they would have been a pretty illustration of the elaborate fashion in which the royal furniture of Egyptian kings 5000 years ago was adorned, and that would have been all. As it was, the excavators cleared the chamber laboriously square inch by square inch, recording the exact position of every tiny fragment; they spent 280 days working there, took hundreds of pages of notes and more than 1000 photographs. From three bits of wooden frame and one panel, shrunk to a sixth of their original size, but preserving traces of the joints, tenons, and mortices, they were able to reconstruct a unique object, the carrying-chair of the queen; the gold hieroglyphs, assembled according to the position in which they lay on the floor, formed groups which could be arranged so as to give sense, proper texts which decorated the upright panels of the chair; and the chair which was built up with new wood and the ancient gold was an exact replica of the vanished original. From the other remains of gold and wood the same painful methods recovered an elaborate arm-chair, a jewel-box, and a bed; but after all had been removed from the tomb the work of reconstruction took Dr Reisner's men two whole years.

A somewhat similar piece of furniture was the sledge-chariot of Queen Shub-ad, found at Ur. Quite unexpectedly there appeared, standing upright in the earth, a gold lion's mask about four inches across, below which was a sort of beard made of bits of shell and lapis lazuli inlay, the latter loose and ready to fall at a touch, so that they had to be secured at once with hot wax. A second similar head was found a little to the right, and a third equidistant on the left; cutting away the soil between them we found, an inch or so further back, a strip of mosaic, tiny squares and triangles of shell and red stone, also loose, but forming a more or less straight line; clearly all these had been attached to a wooden background which had entirely disappeared, and were the decoration of an important object. Higher up and further back another strip of mosaic came to light and another row of gold heads, this time much smaller and in rounder relief, heads of lions and bulls; then on each side vertical bands of mosaic in white and blue, and more strips at right angles, running back into the unexcavated soil. We put forward various theories as to what the object could be, a throne or a chest, but the main problem was what to do with it. Since everything was loose in the earth, and nothing was on the same plane, it was necessary to remove one part before we could get at the next, and the danger was that thereby the design of the whole thing would be lost. It was obvious that whatever the shape had been, the woodwork had been crushed by the weight of earth, and any one measurement might be deceptive; only a very elaborate system of measurement could possibly suffice for a restoration. Each strip of mosaic, however imperfect, was solidified with wax and muslin, and by a multiplicity of notes and scale drawings its exact position in relation to every other fragment was fixed, and then it was lifted out, and the way cleared for getting back to the next bit of ornament. The far side of the chariot was of course approached from behind, and we had to be on the look-out for bands of black powder, the bitumen in which the shell and lapis mosaic had been set, and as this far side had collapsed inwards, and everything stood askew, the bands were not easy to recognize or follow, and we had to determine how much of this angle was original and how much due to accident; I cannot say that our field-notes were as voluminous as Dr Reisner's, but they ran to a great many pages before the last bit of the chariot decoration had been removed. When, from all the measurements taken, a restoration of the chariot was worked out on paper, the total margin of doubt was found to be only just over half an inch; it was possible to build up a new body in modern wood and set in it the old inlay and be sure that this was, within that narrow margin, a faithful reproduction of the original which had decayed to nothing 5000 years before.

It was by a similar process that the gold and mosaic lyres from the cemetery at Ur were preserved, and the copper statues of cattle from al 'Ubaid; these had been made of thin metal hammered over wood, and the wood had gone to dust and the copper was crushed and broken into small fragments and when unearthed was so soft that much of it could be scraped away as powder by the finger; nothing but paraffin wax and muslin would have held them together for transport. Wax is an extraordinarily useful thing in archaeological work, and it has the great advantage of being simple to use. In the case, for instance, of the skeletons of the people who lived at Ur just after the Flood: the bones were flattened by the weight of fifty feet or so of earth, and where they were not reduced to

powder were splintered to atoms, yet the bodies
kept much of their shape, and were material
invaluable for the anthropologist. As much soil
as possible was scraped and brushed away and
then boiling wax was ladled generously over
the skeleton and the soil round it – the only
difficulty was that the earth was so damp, at the
bottom of a pit into which the sun seldom
shone, that the wax tended to form a skin over
it instead of sinking in – and then linen dipped
in hot wax was laid over the body and pressed
well down to fix it to the firm wax below. When
the entire skeleton was duly shrouded the earth
below it was cut away until it rested on three or
four slender columns and could be tilted over
on to a board covered with cotton wool laid
alongside to receive it. The mass of earth adhering to what had been the under side was next
cleaned off and the process of waxing and
shrouding was repeated; wholly encased in
waxed muslin, the body, hardly more than an
inch thick, but rigid, and so light that it could
be carried balanced on one hand, was ready for
packing and despatch to London. There the
upper coat of linen was steamed off, the super-
fluous wax first scraped and then washed away
with benzine, the more discoloured bones

bleached with peroxide of hydrogen and hard-
ened, if necessary, with cellulose or gum damar,
and the skeleton could be shown exactly as it
had been found, with not one of its crumbled
and splintered bones disturbed.

In Mesopotamia a very different problem is
presented by the written tablets which are so
precious a part of the archaeologist's spoils. Very
often they are of unbaked clay and, buried in
damp soil, have become as soft as cheese; softer,
because their material is more homogeneous,
than the earth which clings to them. It would
be impossible to clean them without obliterat-
ing the incised signs which give them their
value; if they are simply kept as they are, they
are likely to crack or even fall to powder, since
the clay is generally impregnated with salt, and
would certainly not stand the shocks of transport; moreover, it is important for the field
worker to know as soon as may be what information they may give – dates, names of buildings
or of kings, to guide him in his work. At Ur any
lumps of clay looking like tablets are lifted from
the ground still encased in their covering of
earth, and are packed in metal boxes filled with
clean sand; after they have been left for a few
days to give the clay a chance to dry, the boxes

are put into a rough-and-ready kiln heated by vaporized crude oil and are baked until the tins are red-hot and the clay is turned into terra-cotta. Then the tablets are taken out; their colour may have altered, which matters little, but they are hard and strong; broken bits can be stuck together, the faces can be cleaned by brushing without any risk to the legibility of the characters; no inscription, however fragmentary, can be overlooked, and its preservation is assured.

The work that one does on an object in the field is only preliminary, just what is necessary to remove it in safety and to keep its component parts together; the preparation of it for exhibition is often a far more complicated task, and can be undertaken only in a museum laboratory where proper facilities exist and chemical processes can be carried out. If the excavator is not qualified to do the work of repair himself, he must at least have some knowledge of how that work will be done, and will plan out his own part accordingly, as otherwise the measures he adopts to preserve his object may seriously interfere with its restoration. In fact, field treatment ought to be reduced to a minimum, so as to leave the laboratory expert with a free hand; at the same time the nature of the object may, as I have shown above, call for treatment involving no small amount of labour in the field, and the archaeologist's first duty is to preserve.

CHAPTER V

The Use of Archaeological Material

*

IN describing the methods of salving antiquities, I have emphasized rather the importance of individual objects, and while the
excavation is actually in progress the archaeologist's attention is necessarily devoted to each
individual object in turn; as soon as it is over he
has to consider his discoveries collectively, and
what were museum exhibits become units in a
series out of which history has to be made. We
have been dealing with a cemetery which presumably contains a large number of graves;
possibly we know the approximate date of the
earliest and the latest burials, or one of them;
in any case the cemetery must have been in use
for a considerable length of time and therefore
ought by its contents to illustrate the modifications of culture which took place during that
time; very likely there were no dates known at

all when the dig began, and the objects from the graves are the only material we possess for the history of a long period; how then is the archaeologist to use his material?

Remember that as we go further back into the past, and our knowledge becomes more scanty, we have to deal in bigger time units; for archaeology a century is a very short span, but a century then may have seen as many changes as a century now. The digger might lump together all that his graves have produced and say, quite fairly, that the collection as a whole illustrates a period of perhaps 300 years; but in that case no single age within that 300 year limit is correctly illustrated by the assembled objects. English life in 1650 was very different from what it was in 1900. A visitor from Mars seeing a great collection of English domestic objects, costumes, etc., ranging in date from 1650 to 1900, but all mixed up together, could get a general idea of a moderately high level of civilization, but could not picture what the setting of life was like at any particular date; if the things were put in historical order our Martian, assuming that he were reasonably intelligent, could not only visualize each period but could trace the course of invention and evolution throughout three

centuries. That is precisely what the archaeologist tries to do.

Where inscribed documents are found the
history produced by digging may be extraordinarily detailed. At Meroe, in the Sudan,
Dr Reisner excavated a number of pyramid
tombs which had escaped the notice of less
methodical diggers; inscriptions showed that
they were the graves of Ethiopian kings and
queens. Now for a short time, about the seventh
century B.C., Egypt was ruled by Ethiopian
Pharaohs; their names were recorded, but nothing was known as to how this conquering
dynasty developed in its original southern home
nor what happened to it after it was again
driven out of Egypt, nor by what process there
evolved out of it the Graecized royal house of
Candace which ruled Ethiopia in the days of
the apostle St Philip. Dr Reisner was able to put
all his tombs in chronological order and to work
out the genealogical tree of the entire family; as
the result of a single excavation a complete
chapter of ancient history could be written for
the first time, and the growth of a civilization
which at one time dominated Egypt could be
traced in detail. One can see how in this remote
corner of central Africa there long persisted the

primitive culture which in prehistoric days had been that of the lower valley of the Nile, how it was brought up against historic Egypt and re-acted to the more advanced civilization of the North until up-to-date organization enabled the Ethiopians to conquer their degenerate teachers by force of arms. One can see how African inconstancy was unable long to hold what brute force had won, how the Negro love of foreign novelty made Ethiopia welcome Greek art, and spread an Alexandrian veneer over the essential barbarism of the Sudan; from the pyramids of Meroe, each reflecting in its furniture the contacts of the moment, there emerges the psychology of a race as well as the politics of many of its generations.

But supposing that there are no written records to define the order of our discoveries, what then? Then the archaeologist is thrown back on his own resources; he has to deduce the order from the facts which he has observed and it is on the fullness and accuracy of his notes that the value of his results will depend. In my last chapter I remarked that the attribution of a pot to the wrong grave might upset an entire system of chronology; that is perhaps putting the matter strongly, but it is quite certain that unless the attributions are generally correct no chronology can ever be worked out. But it is not a question of tomb-groups only; every point in which one grave differs from another may prove to be evidence for relative dating, and must be brought into the argument; because nothing is known nothing must be neglected.

Where the number of graves is large, and the objects from them are numerous, it will generally be possible to recognize with tolerable certainty an earlier and a later group. In some classes of objects there are sure to be signs of development of technique, of the gradual conventionalizing and degeneration of ornamental motives, of the evolution of vase types, and extreme instances of any such process may be taken as dating evidence for particular graves. Sometimes this modification in the contents of the graves may correspond with their position in the cemetery, and it will be clear that the latter expanded in a regular fashion, either along a line or outwards from a centre, and then the plan of the cemetery will become the first basis of classification. Or the evidence may be more direct, as in the great cemetery at Ur, where very often the graves lie one directly

below another in a series which may number
half a dozen separate burials; obviously the
lower grave must in every case be older than the
upper, and wherever the series of superimposed
graves is fairly long the lowest of all is likely to
date fairly early in the period represented by
the cemetery as a whole, and the topmost is
likely to be reasonably late in the same period.
This is the one certain fact on which all future
argument must be based.

The archaeologist first analyses in tabular
form the sum of his field notes; in parallel
columns he will have the number of each grave,
its depth, character, direction, and all its contents symbolized by type numbers – then he can
proceed to make his comparisons. Taking first
the score or so of graves which by their position
at the bottom of a series he knows to be relatively early, he compares their contents, and
will probably find that they have a good deal in
common – that the same types of clay vessels
and the same forms of weapons or tools appear
in many of them. Then, taking the score or so
of late graves, he may find again that there is a
certain similarity between them, but that the
pottery types of the early graves, and the metal
forms, do not re-appear, or re-appear seldom,

in the late graves, while the forms which charac-
terize the latter are wanting in the early group.
If he can establish that fact he is on fairly sure
ground. Assuming that his two groups do represent approximately the beginning and the end
of his cemetery period, he will go on to examine
in the light of their contents the rest of his
graves. Graves which contain only forms regarded as early will be added to the first group;
those with some early types mixed up with
others about which nothing is as yet known will
provisionally be classed together as marking a
step forward in time; those in which early types
are outnumbered by unknown types will be
attributed to the next phase of advance.
Similarly with the later groups; according as
types agree wholly or in part, graves will be
attributed to the last or to the penultimate
phases of the period which the graveyard represents. Perhaps in this way a third of the graves
may be placed in what is hoped to be a chronological grouping, and two-thirds will be left
over as containing types still indeterminate.
These provisional results must then be checked.
The graves of the group supposed to be the
earliest but one, how do they lie in the ground?
Does their depth in relation to the other graves

justify our theory? Do the other contents, beads, gold ornaments, cylinder seals and so on agree with the evidence of the pottery and the bronze tools? If they do, we can assume that we are on the right track, and then the types of vessels and tools found in them but not in the graves of the earliest group of all can be taken as characteristic of their period, and can be used for classifying other graves in which they occur, but the earliest forms are not found at all. Gradually, fresh groups are formed at the expense of the undefined residue of graves left between the early and the late groups, and with fresh evidence arising from each new classification, that undefined residue is in time reduced to nothing, and the whole cemetery is classified in a series of groups of graves which follow a really chronological order and illustrate a rational process of evolution; we still cannot date our periods in terms of years, but we can follow the changes of fashions in things, and therefore in the habits of people, and can attribute any object, by its style, to a definite place in a historical sequence.

Then begins a further correlation. On building sites we have found the remains of houses lying one above the other, each level producing its harvest of broken clay pots, copper utensils and what not. Comparing these with what our cemetery has given us, we may be able to connect various building strata with the sequence-periods of the graves; then for each phase we shall have something of the conditions of living as well as the habits of burial; if, in the building strata, there are ruins of temples, we can add elements of religious ritual and belief.

Just as, in the process of excavation, the archaeologist requires the help of the architect for the reconstruction of his buildings, and of the epigraphist for the reading of his inscriptions, if such be found, so, too, a measure of team-work is necessary for dealing with the mass of material of all sorts which excavation provides for the reconstruction of social life. The complaint is often made that archaeological publications are intolerably dull and consist of masses of undigested detail which cannot possibly interest anyone other than an archaeologist; the answer to this is that the book is not meant for general consumption; conscious that he cannot himself exhaust his subject, the excavator, while putting his own conclusions on record, offers to other specialists the whole of the material evidence on which those conclusions are based, and invites further study; it may be long before the last word has been written, but in the end there will emerge from that chaos of disconnected facts the history which justifies everything. The graves, for instance, will have produced a number of human skulls and skeletons; the anthropologist will take charge of them, and from their physical characteristics determine the racial connexions of the original people and perhaps trace the advent of new stocks, and the relative dating for that advent may coincide with the appearance of new fashions in weapons or pottery; the evidence of disease, arthritis, abscesses in the teeth and so on, will help to explain life conditions, and the setting of broken bones or marks of trepanning will illustrate the surgical knowledge of the period. Figures in stone or clay, drawings on pots or engravings on metal may give some idea of the looks and dress of the people; remains of cloth – sometimes only the impression preserved on metal of cloth whose substance has perished – will show their skill in weaving, and spindle-whorls, loom-weights, and combs will illustrate its process; the constant recurrence in the graves of a long pin lying near the shoulder and parallel with the bone of the upper arm will prove that the outer garment was an unshaped and unsewn shawl or cloak wrapped round the body under one arm and fastened by the pin over the other, a brooch under the chin will mean a shaped gown open at the neck, the remains of a belt will add to the picture which, with knowledge of materials and some idea of styles, we can begin to form. Preserved in their original order, bracelets, necklaces, and head-dresses reproduce rather than suggest the past. The elaborate head-dresses worn at Ur by the court dames of the period of the royal tombs are by now familiar – in the Sargonid age, about 2300 B.C., they have given place to simple ribbons of gold; had these been purchased in the market they would have told us nothing, but found in position they show how two long plaits with gold coiled about them were brought from behind the ears and fixed one above the other across the forehead. Such early Sumerian pictures of men as we possess show them generally clean-shaven, sometimes with long hair, and it was long supposed that the latter must be of a different race. In the graves of the royal cemetery the men commonly wear a head-band made up of two lengths of gold or silver chain and heavy beads of lapis and gold secured behind by a string; now this can only be an early form of the modern Arab 'ageyl', or head-rope, which holds in position the head-cloth worn over the clean-shaven skull; we can fairly argue that the old Sumerian was shaven and wore a head-cloth. But in one grave, whereas the body had the normal head-band, quite apart in a corner of the coffin there was a heap of light brown dust still keeping the texture of hair, and on it lay a plain gold fillet and in it were two spiral hair-rings of gold; on certain occasions the shaved Sumerian wore a wig, just such a cere-monial wig as is represented in the wonderful gold helmet of Mes-kalam-dug found in the same cemetery. Then in graves, again, we find articles of the toilet, tweezers, *kohl*-sticks for painting the eyes, *kohl*-boxes, and whole sets of unguent-vases in alabaster (these in Egyptian tombs), and in Mesopotamia cockle-shells with paint of various colours; we feel that we know the looks of these long-dead folk, something too of their tastes and ideas. We have actual specimens of their handicrafts, objects in metal, stone, and clay, which not only fulfilled a certainable needs and served as a means of self-expression, but may indirectly guide us to fresh knowledge. The geologist will try to trace the sources from which were derived the raw

materials, often imported from abroad, of the
manufactured goods; foreign connexions and
trade routes become manifest. Etruscan graves
in Italy, Crimean barrows, graves in Syria and
Hungary show how the traders in Baltic amber
pushed their business into the far South: the
tools and weapons of the royal cemetery at Ur
are of bronze, containing a certain percentage
of nickel, and as the only ore known to contain
nickel in that proportion comes from Oman, on
the Persian gulf, we can safely assume that it
was from Oman that the Sumerians of 2700 B.C.
derived the metal for their foundries, while the
lapis lazuli, which they employed so freely for
ornaments, came from the Pamir mountains,
N.W. of India. Below the deposit of sand left
by the Flood we found two beads of amazonite,
a green stone for which the nearest known
source is in the Nilghiri hills of Central India,
or in the mountains beyond Lake Baikal – and
at once there is called up the astonishing picture
of antediluvian man engaged in a commerce
which sent its caravans across a thousand miles
of mountain and desert from the Mesopotamian valley into the heart of India. Bones
found in the midden-heaps of houses, or scattered on their floors, will tell the naturalist

what breeds of domestic animals were kept, what wild animals were hunted and eaten; the dried contents of store-jars or pots of offerings will show what grains and what fruits were grown and used for food, while arrows of special types, fish-hooks and net-sinkers, hoes, plough-shares, sickles, and grindstones illustrate the manner in which the hunter and the farmer played their part. If written documents be forthcoming with which the epigraphist can deal, much more may be learnt of social organization and of positive chronology, but even without that, the comparison of the contents of different strata ought to bring out the main vicissitudes of a city's life, as well as the slower process of development and decay.

But here one must strike a warning note. However fruitful in discoveries an excavation may have been and however well the digger has performed his multifarious tasks he must never think that he can say the last word on the subject. He has been working, let us say, on a town site whose well-defined strata cover a long period of time, and in the light of them he can work out a rational scheme of history. But what is true of his town need not be true of a quite near-by neighbour; the political influences that affected one may have left the other untouched. If, as is generally the case, he has dug only part of the site, his evidence is partial and further digging might have modified his conclusions; or, again, his stratification, seemingly complete, may by some accident omit an entire cultural phase, either because the people of that phase did not occupy the part of the city which he has dug or because a wholesale clearance of the site by the builders of the succeeding phase has destroyed the evidence that once was there. Thus at Tell Tay'inat in the Hatay an eighth-century Syro-Hittite palace is built directly on the top of ruins of the fourth millennium B.C.; the same is true of Tell Halaf in northern Mesopotamia, where appearances did mislead the excavators. If one relied upon the evidence of Ur one would conclude that the primitive al 'Ubaid period was of relatively short duration, seeing that it was represented by not more than five levels; but at Eridu, twelve miles away, sixteen temples have been found one above the other and all are of al' Ubaid date! A single excavation is not likely to yield a complete or a continuous record, but by the time a number of sites have been dug the sum of the results worked out by the field archaeologist and his collaborators will be a genuine addition to history. Today we can read, as our grandfathers could not, the story, vivid and circumstantial, of civilizations newly unearthed and of epochs in man's experience which until recently were literally 'dark ages'; and realizing that of all this we have perhaps no contemporary written evidence, or virtually none, some may have been inclined to doubt its value, mistrusting the imagination which seems to base so much on a few potsherds. There must be imagination if life is to be breathed into the dry bones of a dead civilization, but imagination has not been allowed to run riot; the value of the 'few potsherds' as documents for the building-up of history depends, as I have tried to show, on the scientific methods which the archaeologist employs in his work; accurate observation and faithful record are preliminary to any reconstruction.

The prime duty of the field archaeologist is to collect and set in order material with not all of which he can himself deal at first hand. In no case will the last word be with him; and just because that is so his publication of the material must be minutely detailed, so that from it others may draw not only corroboration of his views but fresh conclusions and more light. Should

he not then stop at this? It might be urged that
the man who is admirably equipped to observe
and record does not necessarily possess the
powers of synthesis and interpretation, the
creative spirit and the literary gift which will
make of him a historian. But no record can ever
be exhaustive. As his work in the field goes on,
the excavator is constantly subject to impress-
ions too subjective and too intangible to be
communicated, and out of these, by no exact
logical process, there arise theories which he can
state, can perhaps support, but cannot prove:
their truth will depend ultimately on his own
calibre, but, in any case, they have their value
as summing up experiences which no student of
his objects and his notes can ever share. Granted
that the escavator is adequate to his task, the
conclusions which he draws from his own work
ought to carry weight, and he is bound to put
them forward; if they are palpably wrong then
his observations also may justly be held suspect.
Between archaeology and history there is no
fenced frontier, and the digger who will best
observe and record his discoveries is precisely he
who sees them as historical material and rightly
appraises them: if he has not the power of
synthesis and interpretation he has mistaken his

calling. It is true that he may not possess any literary gifts, and that, therefore, the formal presentation of results to the public may be better made by others; but it is the field archaeologist who, directly or indirectly, has opened up for the general reader new chapters in the history of civilized man; and by recovering from the earth such documented relics of the past as strike the imagination through the eye, he makes real and modern what otherwise might seem a far-off tale.

INDEX OF PROPER NAMES

INDEX OF PROPER NAMES